"Hallman is marvelous as a journalist-storyteller, imbuing Sam's tale with an insightful, human, and compassionate timbre. He takes readers inside Sam's experience and his parents' difficulties while subtly raising questions about our society: Why are we so set on judging each other by looks? What kind of future awaits Sam with his generous heart and incisive mind hidden behind a deformed face? What possibilities exist when science and faith intersect? The true story of a boy with more courage than should be required of anyone, *Sam* is a heartbreaking tale with no easy answers, a story that earns every tear it wrings."

—*Los Angeles Times Book Review*

"Tom Hallman, Jr., won every top journalism prize for writing including the Pulitzer Prize, when he told the gripping story of a teenager, Sam Lightner, who was born with a horrific growth that disfigured his face. This book is even more emotionally powerful than the series, which generated more than 10,000 letters and e-mails to the newspaper. . . . What makes this book so memorable is Hallman's ability to help us see beyond Sam's appearance to the person he is. This is a story about a boy's heart, not his face, and the universal fear of feeling different."

—*The Des Moines Register*

"Gripping . . . Compelling drama, driven by Hallman's factual narration of events."          —*Rocky Mountain News*

"His story is worth hearing."          —*Detroit Free Press*

D0348727

# sam

## the boy behind the mask

Tom Hallman, Jr.

*Tom Hallman*

Berkley Books, New York

A Berkley Book
Published by The Berkley Publishing Group
A division of Penguin Group (USA) Inc.
375 Hudson Street
New York, New York 10014

PRINTING HISTORY
G. P. Putnam's Sons edition / October 2002
Berkley trade paperback edition / October 2003
Berkley trade paperback edition ISBN: 0-425-19174-5

The Library of Congress has catalogued the G. P. Putnam's Sons edition as follows:

Hallman, Tom, date.
Sam : the boy behind the mask / Tom Hallman.
    p.    cm.
ISBN 0-399-14933-3
1. Lightner, Sam, 1985– 2. Face—Abnormalities—
Patients—Biography. 3. Face—Abnormalities—Surgery.
4. Head—Abnormalities—Patients—Biography.
5. Head—Abnormalities—Surgery. 6. Disfigured
children—Biography. I. Title.
RD763.L54 H35     2002              2002069753
362.1'9752'092—dc21
[B]

Printed in the United States of America

10   9   8   7   6   5   4   3   2   1

TO BARBARA SCHULD HALLMAN

She hears the stories first.

# contents

# sam the boy behind the mask

# the mask

*The serial number of a human
specimen is the face, that accidental
and unrepeatable combination
of features. It reflects neither
character nor soul, nor what we
call the self. The face is only the
serial number of a specimen.*

MILAN KUNDERA,
*Immortality*

1  A movie flickers on the screen set up in front of the chalk-
   board, but almost none of the twenty-eight eighth-graders
pay attention. Under cover of darkness, they talk about the plan for
tonight, in restless teenage voices that bounce around the second-
floor classroom at Gregory Heights Middle School in Portland,
Oregon.

   Their teacher looks up and clears his throat as a warning. The
conversations continue at a whisper. Only one student, sitting in
the last row—at five feet and eighty-three pounds the smallest in the
class—remains silent. Sam Lightner never draws undue attention to
himself. He moves like smoke. Perhaps it's because he didn't speak
until he was four years old. He had to learn how to force air through
the hole a doctor cut in his throat when he was born. All his life,
people have assumed his silence meant he was retarded.

Sam's an excellent student, an honor student, already tackling high-school-level geometry. He's a keen observer, listening to conversations but not joining in, letting people forget that he's there. Over the years, Sam has learned that people often don't listen to what he's saying because his face distracts them. He was three years old when he realized he was different. He'd been running in a hallway at home when he saw his reflection in a full-length mirror. He touched the left side of his face, almost to prove whether he was in fact that little boy. And then he sat down on the floor and cried.

Sam stares at the screen from his one good eye, and takes notes on the making of the U.S. Constitution. He always takes accurate notes, and shares them willingly. Other students can count on him when they do projects together. Although the desk swallows his frail frame, Sam is in the best shape of his life. Yet whenever the bell rings and other boys stampede to the door, Sam stands to the side so he doesn't get trampled.

Today, his class is consumed with the open house that Grant High School is holding for the city's eighth-graders, incoming freshmen, the class of 2004. Sam figures his classmates feel the way he does—a bit nervous with the move from the warm cocoon of this middle school to the rough-and-tumble world of hormones, dates, and competitive popularity. He knows his homeroom teacher, Mr. Hartinger, is worried about him, concerned that Sam might not survive at inner-city Grant, Portland's biggest high school.

Most adults worry about Sam. They can't help pitying the boy. When he was a baby, strangers asked his mother if she'd taken drugs while pregnant. Once a girl called him an "ugly baby." As he grew, people told him they'd pray for him. Others shook their heads and turned away. Adults see themselves in Sam. They remember the children they once were. They wonder where he finds the strength to deal with his life.

Sam just gets up each day and goes out into the world and learns to ignore most of what he hears. When his parents sat down and talked with him about the facts of life, it had to do not with sex, but with him. They told him that this thing on the side of his face made him look different, but that inside he was like any other boy. They told him to never forget that truth. They have always treated Sam as they do their other children. When he doesn't listen, he gets in trouble. He has chores. His face has never been an excuse for him to be lazy or to feel sorry for himself.

But it's the little things, the things people around him take for granted, that Sam longs for. To be able to walk into a room and not have anyone stare at him. To be able to play dodge ball at the end of Boy Scout meetings and not have anyone *really* throw the ball at him out of fear of hitting his face. As much as Sam hates being stared at, he despises being pitied.

When the movie is over, Sam hears two boys near him talking about trying out for Grant's basketball team, and that makes him sad. Sam knows he will never play sports. He will always be a spectator. Some girls to his left are talking about what they will wear tonight, and how they hope their outfits will impress the boys. He wishes people would notice what he wears.

Sam has spent the last four days in this February 2000 carefully choosing what to wear. He's discarded one shirt after another, trying for the right combination with the pants hanging in his closet. But it doesn't matter. Sam could show up in the latest fashion, and still, he knows, no girl would swoon over him.

Tonight, he simply wants to blend in, to be like everybody else. He knows that will be impossible.

Suddenly Sam drops his pencil. He fights to breathe. A ragged burst of air escapes from the hole in his throat—the tracheostomy allows air to funnel directly into his lungs, bypassing the swollen tissue that blocks the usual airway. His classmates turn to look at him. Casually, to avoid attracting any more attention, Sam drops his head and coughs, attempting to clear the blockage. Nothing. He snaps his head back and wheezes.

Mr. Hartinger gets up from his desk. Every teacher in the school has been trained to help Sam, but he hates being helped. He waves Mr. Hartinger away, then stands and backs out of the classroom. He uses the weight of his body to close the door, and his violent coughing now echoes through the empty hall. Sam's airway remains blocked, filled with mucus and fluids that flow from a vascular system gone awry, a condition that has puzzled doctors from the moment he was born.

He moves down a set of steps, holding the handrail to keep his balance, then toward the main office, where a portable suction device is kept for him.

"Hi, Sam," the principal's secretary says when he opens the door. "Are you okay?"

Sam forces a nod. Sometimes he loses the struggle with his mouth and tongue to shape words. He finds it easier simply to shake his head.

He rummages through a shelf, looking for the brown grocery bag he has carried from home. From inside he pulls out a blue nylon case the size of a small lunch pail. He tucks it under his arm and steps quickly into the hall, taking care to slip past the nurse's office. If she sees him with the blue case she'll ask questions.

Sam turns left and goes into the boys' bathroom, where he bends to peer under the stalls. When he's sure he's alone, he walks to the sink, unzips the case, and uncoils a tube that looks like a small vacuum cleaner hose. Attached to one end is a thin white nozzle. He guides the nozzle into a piece of plastic at the hole in his throat. He activates the machine. A hum fills the room, and the device clears his airway. Sam sucks in a deep breath and coughs. When he feels he is breathing normally, he removes the nozzle and replaces the tube in the case.

He pauses to study his face in the mirror, to see what others see when they look at him.

A huge mass of flesh balloons from the left side of his face. The main body of tissue, laced with blue veins, swells in a dome from sideburn level to chin. The mass draws his left eye into a slit, warps his mouth into a small inverted half-moon. It looks as though someone had slapped three pounds of wet clay onto his face, where it clings, burying the boy inside.

But his right eye is clear and perfectly formed. His iris is a deep, penetrating brown, and the third of his face surrounding this normal eye gives the impression of a normal teenager. Sam's close-cropped hair is shaped carefully, trimmed neatly behind his delicate right ear. His right cheek glows with the blushing good health that the rest of his face has obscured.

There is the mask.

And there is the boy behind the mask.


The last school bell rings, and students crowd out of classrooms and jam the halls. They gather in front of lockers to talk, they shout and make plans for the afternoon.

Sam slips through them unnoticed. He bangs his locker shut and exits through a side door. A basketball game is under way on a court outside, but Sam doesn't join in. He likes shooting baskets with his friends, but his head makes it hard for him to maintain his balance in a real game, where players are pushed and collide.

He heads home on a winding street. In good weather, when people might sit outside or children might play on front lawns, Sam hears laughter as he passes. He wonders whether people are laughing at him. He never knows. But he assumes the worst. It's cold today, and the streets are empty. No one stares at him until he reaches a busy intersection. Yesterday, at this same intersection, someone in a car rolled down the window and yelled at him: *"Freak!"*

When he got home, he didn't tell his parents about the taunt. It stung, but he never reacted, never even let on to the man in the car that he'd heard. Sam has learned from his parents to do that. They've heard comments since the day he was born. There are moments when Sam forgets his face. He'll be thinking about motorcycles, about getting his learner's permit to drive, about girls. And then someone says something, or turns away or gapes in horror. Then Sam remembers that no matter what he thinks or feels, people see him only as some kind of monster. Every day, he hears someone mention his face. There are the cruel comments—"weird"—and there are those uncomfortable silences that fall across the restaurant or the movie theater lobby when he appears. He doesn't cry or act embarrassed. He stares straight ahead and goes about his business.

Sam knows he looks odd. The left side of his face is a swollen mass that resembles a pumpkin rotting in the fields after Halloween. He doesn't mind so much the children who stare, naturally curious about a boy who looks different from them. It's older children and adults who make him mad. A girl once followed him through a grocery store, staring at him. He turned on her, made the scariest face he could, and laughed when she ran to her mother. Sometimes there's nothing he can do. A few weeks ago, at home, he heard footsteps on the front porch. From the dining room he saw a neighbor boy and two kids he didn't recognize. They knocked on the front door. Sam's mother went to answer, and the neighbor kid said he was looking for Sam's brother. But Sam watched as all three of the boys peered around his mother, trying to get a glimpse of him, as if he were a specimen in the zoo. Once again, the neighbor boy had brought visitors to the Lightners' to show them the kid with the weird face. This time, through the window, Sam's eyes met the boys' eyes. They turned and walked off the porch. Sam saw them run, laughing, across the street. If only they knew him, knew how funny he was, how much he liked watching sports, and playing on the computer. Sam has learned that adults are often nicer to him than are children his own age.

Sam is happy when he reaches home. Here he can fight with his brother, tease his sister, and be a fourteen-year-old whose parents have to bug him to keep his room clean. The house is wood-framed, with a wide front porch and cream-colored paint. Like thousands of people on Portland's east side, the Lightners are house-rich; real estate prices here have soared in the last decade. But they need new carpets and appliances, and the mail seems to bring only bills. Sam's mother, Debbie, works part-time as a bank teller, for the health insurance.

Sam walks into the dining room, slings off his backpack, and pulls out a binder. He starts his homework, hoping to finish it before going to the open house tonight, and is still working on it when his mother arrives. Now his brother and sister run into the house. Sam closes his books and joins them in the living room. Emily, twelve, and Nathan, nine, drop to the floor and play cards. Sam watches them, but can't get the open house out of his mind. Grant High will be filled with kids, kids like those who had come to the front door.

The family cat, Alice, jumps onto his lap, and Sam strokes the creature with his thin hands. And then, all at once, he is overcome by an urge to be alone. He lifts the cat off his lap, ignoring a plaintive meow, and goes toward the kitchen, where his mother is washing vegetables at the sink. He stops in the doorway and hesitates. Finally he clears his throat, and forms his words carefully:

"I'm not hungry tonight."

His mother sighs. She turns to look at him, not bothering to turn off the water. Sam sees her studying him, running her eyes over his bony arms as he wearily props himself against the door frame. He knows she's been watching him like this since he left the hospital six months ago. She's scared the mass on the side of his face will once again roar to life and maybe, this time, kill him.

"I'm full," he says.

She bends her head toward him, about to speak. He knows what's coming—the concerns, the worries, all the questions that he doesn't want to answer. He moves to cut her off.

"Really, Mom. I'm full."

He gives her the thumbs-up sign and a smile. After spending his young life trying to make himself understood, Sam has found alternatives to the words that are so hard for him to shape. He uses his good eye and hand gestures to get his point across.

"Okay, Sam," she says quietly.

He leaves the doorway and goes upstairs. He walks along the hall to the door with the toy license plate announcing "Sam." In his room he fiddles with a laptop, leafs through a motorcycle magazine, and plays with a foam basketball.

He sits on the bed and tosses the ball across the room, hitting a poster on the wall. His mother made that poster, assembling family photographs and documents and then laminating them. They are the remnants of a fading childhood.

In the middle of the poster is a questionnaire Sam filled out when he was eight. He had been asked to list his three greatest wishes. First, he said, he wanted $1 million. Next, a dog. On the third line, he doodled three question marks—back then, he couldn't think of anything else he wanted or needed. If he could be granted one wish now, it would be to look better. Not perfect. Not like a model. Sam just wants to look a little more normal. He wants people to see beyond his face.

He hears the back door shut downstairs. His father is home. Sam goes to his door. He can hear his parents talking, and he listens carefully, but he can't make out the words. Maybe his parents are talking about him.

He changes into his clothes for the open house, the shirt and pants he selected with such care. All eighth-graders are obsessed with how they look and how they'll fit in at school. Sam is no different. He watches MTV. He knows what's considered popular and cool. He knows what girls like. Everyone talks about beauty being on the inside, but Sam knows that's only what people tell themselves. It may seem true to little kids, or to men and women in their forties. But to a teenager like Sam, it's a lie.

When Sam was due to arrive at middle school, his fifth-grade teacher, worried that he would be teased and misunderstood, created a slide show on his life. She gathered photographs of Sam from his family, and asked students who knew him in grade school to write letters of introduction. Then she held an assembly at the middle school, and at all the grade schools that would send kids to Gregory Heights. After the students had seen pictures of Sam, she read from letters his schoolmates had written.

"I've known Sam for the greater portion of my time at Rose City Park," one student wrote. "Not very well until this year, though. I remember that kids, ignorant, hateful kids, would make fun of him. . . . Think how horrible it was for him. I, like many other people, did nothing. I was quiet and got my fair share of teasing. . . . I deeply regret [that I did nothing]. I wasn't in Sam's class again until fifth grade. I saw a tremendous improvement in the other kids. Perhaps ignorance was our biggest enemy. I saw a new side of Sam, too. A side that had always been there, a side that only needed a closer look. So I ask you, before you judge Sam, or anyone for that matter, remember that a person's true beauty is not on the outside, but within their heart."

Sam's teacher ended the assemblies by reminding students that while Sam looked different, he was a normal boy. They didn't have to be his best friends, but they should not be afraid of him, or make fun of him.

Life hasn't been perfect for Sam in middle school. Teachers were shocked when they first saw him. When he walked down the halls early on, he knew that a lot of kids and teachers assumed he was a special education student. In time, though, everyone in the school has come to see him as just Sam. They don't care about the disfiguring mass, or at least they don't show it if they do. But high school and beyond, he knows, will be different. No matter what people tell him, Sam recognizes that he is moving into a larger world of judgmental teenagers. And he carries with him a terrible handicap, a face that scares others.

He checks the clock, and sees that it's almost time to go. He takes a deep breath. He hopes he's picked the right clothes. He runs his left hand through his brown hair. He must imagine what he looks like. There's no mirror to examine his face. In this boy's room, there's never been a mirror.

Sam makes his way down the stairs. He's wheezing, breathless, by the time he gets to the bottom. In the kitchen, his father, David, a weathered jewelry designer who saves money by riding a motorcycle to work, is waiting.

"Ready for this, Sam?" David asks.

Sam nods and replies with a garbled sound.

"Okay," his father says. "Then let's go."

Sam and his parents get into a Honda Accord with 140,000 hard miles on the odometer. A few blocks from home, while the car is stopped at a light, Sam senses someone looking at him—he's used to this. A woman walking a dog has caught sight of Sam. She makes no pretense of being polite, doesn't avert her eyes. Even when the light changes, and the car moves, the woman keeps staring, turning her head as if watching a train leave a station.

Grant High's open house attracts more than 1,500 students and parents from throughout the city. Even though they've come early, the Lightners can't find a parking place at the school. David circles the streets until he finds one, several blocks away. Sam and his parents step out of the car and walk through the dark neighborhood.

Debbie asks her son how he's doing. He doesn't answer, doesn't know the *real* answer. It's too complicated, too hard to explain; he just wants to get in the school. As he passes near a streetlight, a dark green Range Rover with five or six teenage boys turns onto the street. One of the boys points at him. The car slows. The windows fill with staring faces and pointing fingers. Sam has run into kids like these before: they think they're so much better than everyone else. The boys in the car laugh at something one of them has said, and then, when they're done teasing Sam, the car moves on. Sam knows his father was about to say something to the kids; he also figures he'll run into the same boys at Grant.

As they near the school, more and more teenagers are in the streets, gathering in packs, chattering nervously. Sam recognizes a girl who goes to his school. He has a secret crush on her. She has brown wavy hair, and a smile that makes his hands sweat and his heart race whenever he sees her. She's alone, and he hurries to catch up with her.

"Hi, Sam," she says.

He nods. "Hi."

His parents lag behind, allowing him some privacy. The girl does most of the talking. Sam's happy just to be next to her, to have a friend to walk into Grant with. Two blocks from the school, Sam notices that the girl discreetly falls behind him.

He slows to match her step. She hurries ahead. She's embarrassed, he realizes, to be seen with him, as if being with him will somehow rub off on her, damage her reputation. He slows again, lets her go and walks on alone.

Tonight there are no shadows for Sam to hide in. Every light is on at the high school. He arrives at the north entrance and stands on the steps, looking in through the windows. Girls cluster and laugh together. Boys huddle under a sign announcing a basketball game. This is no middle school.

Sam grabs the door handle, hesitates for the briefest of moments. He has ridden on a motorcycle at speeds as high as 110 miles per hour, but that wasn't as scary as walking through this door. He pulls the door open and enters, and a wave of sound washes over him. The halls are filled with students, the boys tall and strong-looking, the girls so grown-up. Sam takes two steps into the hallway, and the students turn and stare. His heart races. He wipes the palms of his hands on his pants, but it does no good. Part of him wants to turn and walk out that door, back into the night. But he does not flinch. He looks straight ahead and walks into the school, into noise and laughter and chaos, into the urgency and pain that is all about being fourteen years old and knowing you look different from everyone else.

2    It was September 1985, Debbie Lightner would remember later. She was seven months pregnant, and had just rung up a customer's order, when she felt her baby kick. She had started working at the jewelry store part-time six years before, when she was still in high school, selling diamonds, helping to organize repairs, and learning how to engrave.

Until a few weeks earlier, no one believed she was pregnant, because she had barely gained any weight. But then she grew so rapidly that everyone thought she was about to deliver, even though the due date was still around two months away.

She looked at the clock, saw it was almost noon—time for her doctor's appointment—and went to the back of the store, where her husband, David, did custom work, designing rings, pendants, and bracelets. They had met two years before, when David was hired.

Debbie scheduled her medical appointments at midday, because her doctor's office was in the same mall as the store, and her pregnancy was proving so easy—no morning sickness, no aches and pains—that she could be examined quickly and still have time for lunch.

She and David walked through the mall to the doctor's office, and after only a brief wait were led to an examination room. A few minutes later, her doctor entered, took one look at Debbie, and smiled.

"You *do* look bigger," he said.

Even the receptionist must have noticed, Debbie thought.

"Why don't you lie down for me."

The doctor ran his hands across Debbie's abdomen, then placed one end of a cloth tape measure at the top—where he could feel the baby—and pulled the other end toward her pelvis. At past exams, he'd measured once, stuck the tape measure back in his pocket, and made small talk.

Today he looked puzzled. He took the stethoscope from around his neck and listened. He measured again.

"You're larger than you should be," he muttered, as much to himself as to Debbie.

He measured a third time.

"I don't want you to worry." He patted her on the shoulder. "There's probably nothing wrong. I only hear one heartbeat," he said. "But let's make sure you're not having twins."

"What?" David said.

"Not likely," the doctor told him. "I just want to make sure."

He led Debbie into an adjoining room and helped her onto a table. He wheeled a small machine next to the table.

"I'm going to do an ultrasound," he explained.

Debbie tried to see the screen beside him. The grainy black-and-white image there didn't look anything like a baby. The doctor worked silently, stopping occasionally to measure Debbie's mid-section again.

"Okay," he said. "I'm sure there are not twins in there. But I can't figure out these measurements. Maybe the amniotic fluid's built up—you're about as big as a woman who's close to being full term with twins. I'll schedule you for an ultrasound at the hospital, one better than I can give here. Then we can get a good idea of what's going on."

The next day, as Debbie lay on a table at Emanuel Hospital, she could see her child on the monitor.

"Is that a foot?" she asked.

"That's a foot," said the technician. He pointed at the screen. "This is a hand."

And then he stopped talking. Debbie asked more questions, but the technician just nodded. She looked at David. He shrugged.

The technician pushed a button on the machine, to make pictures of the images on the monitor. Immediately after they slid out on one side, he placed them in a manila folder, which he kept closed under his arm. When the test ended, he quickly excused himself and left with the folder still tucked under his arm.

Debbie and David sat and waited, until there was a knock on the door.

A man in a lab coat entered. "Please come with me," he said. They followed him to an office where another man, sitting behind a desk, stood and introduced himself as a prenatal specialist.

"Have a seat," he said, pointing to the two chairs in front of his desk. He sat down and opened a folder.

"First, do you want to know the sex of your baby?" he asked.

The Lightners shook their heads.

"The reason you're here to see me," he said, "is that the ultrasound revealed a problem with the baby." He paused a moment. "The baby's brain is floating outside the head. That's why you are so big."

The brain . . . how? The Lightners asked.

"There's a hole in the skull and the brain is just outside," the specialist explained. "I am sorry, but there's nothing that can be done." He said he had to be blunt. "This child will die. Some parents would choose to terminate."

The Lightners didn't bother looking at each other. "No," they said in unison.

The specialist regarded them as if he'd pegged them as naive parents who would change their mind in the privacy of their home, when the reality of what was to happen hit them. He chose his next words with care. "There is a very good chance this baby will die at birth. I'm sorry."

There was nothing more he could say. No empty words of encouragement.

"I've called your doctor," he told them. "You should go back to his office now. He'll talk with you about what's next."

The Lightners drove silently to the doctor's office, neither of them daring to talk about the fears they carried in their hearts.

"We won't know anything until this baby is born," the doctor said. "It's a good sign, though that the baby is kicking and moving a lot."

The baby would have to be delivered by cesarean section, he went on, because the brain was exposed. That would be the only hope of saving the child's life. A neurosurgeon would be in the operating room in case anything could be done to tuck the brain back into the skull. Even then, if the child lived, there would be severe brain damage.

"All we can do now is wait," he said.

A few days later, when Debbie Lightner got out of bed in the morning, she felt tension in her lower back. She figured it was stress. The last few days had been horrible, a dashing of dreams and hopes, mourning a child she'd never had a chance to hold in her arms.

Breaking the news to her mother had been especially hard. "The baby has problems," she'd told her on the telephone, and at that moment, the reality hit Debbie in a way that it hadn't in the doctor's office.

This morning her mother called to see how Debbie was holding up. When she heard about the backache, she suggested it might be early labor, but Debbie reminded her that the baby wasn't due for six weeks. Her mother wasn't convinced. When she called back that night she talked David into taking Debbie to the hospital as a precaution.

When they arrived at the hospital, at around nine, a nurse examined Debbie and determined that not only was she in labor, but also she was far enough along to be admitted. The contractions needed to be stopped. Nurses gave Debbie drugs intravenously all night, but her labor continued. By morning, the contractions had increased, and it was obvious that she was going to give birth.

Everything happened fast. Debbie was wheeled to the operating room. A nurse told David that if he wanted to watch, he would have to put on scrubs.

When he reached the operating room, David saw Debbie sitting up wincing. She had felt something sharp in her back. An epidural, the nurse explained, that would numb her for the C-section. The labor, another nurse called out, was moving swiftly. Debbie, who had never been in a hospital before, told the doctor she didn't feel numb.

"Let's hurry," the doctor snapped at the anesthesiologist.

Someone grabbed Debbie's arm, extended it, and stuck her with an intravenous line. She was obviously numb. Someone pulled her left arm and took her blood pressure.

"Isn't a neurosurgeon supposed to be here?" Debbie asked.

"It's okay," a nurse reassured her. "There are a lot of people here. We'll get whatever doctor is needed when the baby comes."

Debbie's arms trembled.

And then she heard a baby cry.

"It's a boy," someone said.

There was a pause, and the sound of machines in the operating room.

"It's not what we thought," the doctor said.

Another pause.

"It's something else."

And then Debbie Lightner passed out.

David Lightner saw one of the nurses lift a baby. He attempted to catch a glimpse of his son. The baby's head seemed to be intact, but something fleshy was hanging off his face: it looked like a water balloon was attached. The nurse backed out of the room with the baby in her arms.

What, David Lightner wondered, was going on?

In the resuscitation room, the nurse placed the baby in a radiant warmer, a sort of basket on wheels. He struggled to breathe. It wasn't just the fact that his lungs weren't developed. The growth on his face was making his struggle even more dangerous. Unless the hospital staff moved swiftly, the child would die.

The nurse now pushed the warmer into a resuscitation room. A doctor inserted a tube into the baby's mouth, to force air into his tiny lungs. The baby kicked. Nurses worked an intravenous line into the baby's navel, to give access to veins and arteries. The baby's blood was then drawn, to monitor the level of carbon dioxide in his lungs.

The baby, now stabilized, was wheeled in the warmer to the Neonatal Intensive Care Unit, and assigned to Nurse Barry Green. Babies fascinated Green, but he'd never seen one like this. If the child was turned to one side, he was a normal, cute newborn. If he was turned to the other, his deformity was hard to believe. The baby had two faces.

David Lightner, still in his scrubs, entered the room. He joined a circle of doctors and nurses looking at his son.

"What is it?" he asked.

"I don't know," one of the doctors answered. He took a sterile cloth and covered the mass on the side of the baby's face with it. "This is what he will look like after he has surgery," the doctor told David. "Remember, this is what he will look like."

The doctor removed the cloth. A nurse took two Polaroid pictures of the baby and handed them to David, and asked for the baby's name. "Sam," he told her.

He took the pictures and went back to the operating room.

"Can I hold him?" Debbie asked.

"No," David said. "He's in Intensive Care. His brain *is* in his skull. That's the good news."

He handed her the pictures, and Debbie saw the bulging growth on the left of her son's face and under his neck. "What is it?"

"I don't know. But he's alive."

Debbie knew what a Down's-syndrome baby looked like, or a baby with a cleft lip. But this was bizarre. She covered the mass on the Polaroid with her finger. Her son was a normal baby. She took her finger off. He was not at all normal.

The next morning, Debbie was taken in a wheelchair to Neonatal Intensive Care. The main furnishings here were isolettes, covered cribs with regulated temperature and oxygen flow. On one was taped a sign with words from Dr. Suess's *Green Eggs and Ham*: "I am Sam, Sam I am." And there in the isolette was her son, a tube in his mouth, wires from a heart monitor snaking out from his chest. Debbie asked if she could hold him. Nurse Green told her Sam was too fragile.

"What is that on his face?" she asked.

Green said he didn't know.

If she couldn't hold him, could she at least touch her son, Debbie wondered. Green lifted the isolette cover, and Debbie reached in. With one finger she touched the mass on Sam's face. It was soft, and jiggled like Jell-O. Her son looked like something in a science fiction movie.

"What is it?" Debbie asked again.

The nurses had wondered too. One had gone to the textbooks for help. She now approached Debbie and handed her a page photocopied from a book.

"Cystic hygroma," Debbie read. She scanned the words, none of which made sense, and then focused on a series of photographs of what looked like lumps on a foot and an arm. There were no pictures of facial deformities.

Green closed the cover to the isolette, and David helped his wife back to her room. When she was alone, she picked up one of the Polaroids her husband had given her. Once again she covered the mass with her fingers to see what her son should have looked like.

She lifted her finger from the photo. She thought about his future, about all sorts of things: Would he have a girlfriend? Would people be afraid of him? Would he be accepted?

And then Debbie Lightner wept.

3   Even though a tube was forcing oxygen into Sam's two-day-old lungs, the mass on the left side of his face hung on his chest and its sheer weight made it even more difficult for his undeveloped lungs to function.

The Intensive Care staff left a message for Tim Campbell, Portland's only private-practice pediatric surgeon. Dr. Campbell was forty-eight years old, a bulky man, built like a football player. He moved slowly, as if his feet ached. With his old-fashioned sayings— "He bled like Billy Sunday," "It's like hauling coal to Newcastle"— he came across as a country doctor accustomed to shooting the breeze on someone's front porch. His fingers were large, more comfortable, it would seem, with a hammer than with a scalpel. And yet nurses swore that when Tim Campbell stood over a patient in the operating room and said it was time to do it, they'd seen a grace they wouldn't have believed possible. He was often called "the miracle worker," because he had helped newborns who weighed even less than a pound.

Campbell wasn't known for his warm bedside manner. He told it like he saw it, never gave false hope to soften a blow. Parents sometimes complained that he was gruff, even brutal. But he got results, and years later those same parents would thank him for what he had done for their child. He received Christmas cards and photographs from patients who wanted to keep in contact with him. His practice thrived because he embraced the hard cases.

He couldn't practice his first love, heart surgery, because he suffered recurrent blood clots in his left leg, and long hours over an operating table had already caused two attacks. So he devoted himself to pediatric surgery.

Campbell was at the hospital when he received the message from the ICU, and soon after was on his way there. He asked for the Lightner file at the front desk, and followed Nurse Green to the baby's isolette. Campbell studied the child. He'd seen plenty of serious cases during his pediatric surgery fellowship in 1960 at Pittsburgh Children's Hospital. For a year he'd done nothing but operate on children, learning how to pay meticulous attention to small bodies. Yet he'd seen nothing like this outside a textbook.

"What is it?" Green asked.

"A vascular anomaly," Campbell said.

"Can't you just cut it off?"

"There's so much invasion. It can't be cut without nerve damage and blood loss."

The anomaly, Campbell explained, was a living mass of blood vessels. It had replaced normal tissue with a tangle of lymphatic capillary cells. In children who have tumors, the tumor recruits new blood vessels and distorts the surrounding tissue. In Sam's case, the malformation developed in the womb; the left side of his face never had a normal structure. The malformation, extending from his ear to his chin, had burrowed deep inside Sam's tissue. Doctors, Campbell said, knew little about what caused such anomalies. It was known that they were composed of fluid-filled cysts and clots varying from microscopic to fingertip-size. And that they were rare. But what this boy had was extremely rare.

*The Surgeon and the Child*, a 1959 book that Campbell considered his Bible, sheds some light on congenital anomalies. Such anomalies, it tells us, are not uncommon. Most can be corrected, or if not harmful, are soon forgotten and become part of the individual. About four percent of infants in the United States are born with deformities that surgeons can correct. But a few—about one percent—are born with such complicated abnormalities that surgeons can offer little more than lifesaving assistance.

Sam Lightner, Campbell understood, was one of these infants.

The odds of an anomaly this extensive, and so treacherously placed, Campbell figured, were about one in a million. He thought of a sentence from *The Surgeon and the Child*: "Our duty as doctors is crystal-clear—to preserve life. And yet, when looking at a hopeless little mass of deformed humanity, compassion wrestles with duty."

He reached into the isolette and gently opened Sam's mouth. The mass swelled up from below and into his tongue. It was preventing his breathing, threatening his life.

Campbell remembered another passage from the book: "It is difficult to measure devotion or to sound the depths of love for a living thing. Those who have been fortunate enough to have been spared the tragedy of a seriously deformed child are incapable of guiding or advising the unfortunate." Campbell had two kids, both healthy.

He stepped back from the isolette, and went to find the Lightners. He knocked on the door to Debbie's room.

He introduced himself as he stepped inside. "I'm not going to hide anything. This is bad news. What your son has is called a hemo-lymphangioma. Think of it as a birthmark. The cystic hygroma part of it is bad enough. But the lymphatic part is real trouble."

David remembered how the doctor in the neonatal ICU had placed a cloth over the mass to show what Sam might look like after an operation. "What about surgery?" he asked.

Campbell shook his head. "I can't do much with that. Your son has a birthmark on the outside and on the inside. It's a giant one, and it's in a bad place."

"So what do we do?" David said.

"He's having a hard time breathing. I'm going to have to operate." He looked at the Lightners, wanting them to understand what he was about to say. "This surgery won't be to change the appearance of Sam's face, but to save his life. And it's not going to be easy. It's going to take a long time. I have to tell you that. But if I don't operate, he's not going to make it."

It did not take long for David and Debbie to give their consent, and the next morning, three days after Sam Lightner was born, Campbell and a team of nurses stood over him in a heated operating room. Because Sam was born premature, his body lacked the ability to maintain a body temperature. The thermostat was hiked to eighty-five degrees.

Campbell started under Sam's neck, where there was less of a vascular component. An infant is not a little adult, and here particularly there was no margin for error. If all the blood in Sam's body were drained, it would barely fill a coffee cup. Slicing a blood vessel in the mass might mean Sam would bleed to death. Sam's face was filled with nerves that controlled facial features. Slicing a nerve here might mean Sam would lose the ability to move his eye or tongue. Campbell had to ignore the heat—he was, understandably, sweating—and proceed as carefully and deliberately as possible. After some six hours, Campbell closed. He had removed one pound, ten ounces of tissue from under Sam's neck.

Campbell met the Lightners afterward. "He's fine," he told them. "He did great. It was long, but I got a lot of the mass off his chin."

He paused.

"But there's nothing I can do about the side of his face. I'm sorry. And I'm going to have to go back in. What's on the floor of his mouth is closing around his airway, and if I don't do something, he's not going to be able to breathe."

Days later, Campbell operated a second time, to create a hole in Sam's throat and remove some of the bulk above his left ear. He looked once more at the side of Sam's face. More surgery, he decided, was too dangerous. The two surgeries had sliced away a quarter of Sam's weight already.

Dr. Campbell closed the Lightner file. He had done all he could for this boy.

**4** Debbie Lightner held her son in her arms and said good-bye. He was in no shape to go home. She gently lay him back in his isolette and kissed him.

Sam would have to live at the hospital for at least two months. Debbie stared down at this little bundle, his jaw twisted, his tongue sideways in his mouth. She had held him to her breast, but he had been unable to feed. Now he had so many lines running from his body: IV lines, a heart monitor, a tube pumping nourishment directly to his stomach.

When she left the hospital, she felt as if she were abandoning her son. She returned to work at the jewelry store and showed photographs of Sam to her co-workers. They all found something nice to say. No one mentioned the face. They focused on his nose or his tiny fingers.

The day after Christmas 1985, the Lightners brought Sam home from the hospital. The homecoming was not at all what they had planned. The hospital refused to release him unless a nurse rode home in the car with the Lightners and lived with them. Sam was still fragile, and life with him would be difficult, the doctors and nurses emphasized, nothing they could handle on their own. There would be no parenting books to turn to for reassurance. Even other parents wouldn't be able to relate.

No one slept that first night. Sam had to be fed every two hours through the tube that ran to his stomach. The nurse fed him, but Debbie was at her side. The Lightners soon tired of the nurses, who rotated in shifts. As nice as they were, they only served to remind the couple of Sam's problems. They couldn't be a true family with a nurse hanging around the house.

Debbie called the insurance company.

"I'm home to take care of my baby," she told a representative of the company. "We don't want a nurse. We don't need a nurse. We can do this."

The representative was sympathetic but cautious.

"I'm his mother," Debbie continued. "Let me be his mother."

The company eliminated the day-shift nurse. And then the second shift. The last to go was the night nurse. Seven months after Sam Lightner was born, Debbie and David had the chance to be full-time parents. As they climbed into bed the first night without a nurse, they heard Sam moving and the sound of bursts of air through the baby monitor on the nightstand. He couldn't cry or laugh, he couldn't control the flow of air through the hole in his throat.

Although they had never discussed it, both Sam's parents knew that they wouldn't hide their son from the world. When he was a little older, Debbie pushed Sam in his stroller at the mall and watched people come her way. One person and then another would spot Sam, and discreet glances or outright stares would ensue. At first it angered her. Then it saddened her. When David saw this happen, he felt like running over and punching the gawkers. But he and Debbie couldn't live like that. If they reacted to every stare, what message would they be giving Sam as he grew older and faced the world?

And so they ignored the stares. Friends and relatives followed their lead, striving for normalcy. Debbie's best friend offered to babysit, and had Debbie teach her how to suction out Sam's tracheostomy tube when it became clogged, as if it were a routine procedure in any household.

The hole in his throat made it impossible for the growing boy to speak. When he was eighteen months old, a nurse who worked with Sam's pediatrician told the Lightners about a program in which social workers provided services to special-needs children who would eventually enter the Portland public schools. Debbie had Sam evaluated, and a teacher recommended he be taught sign language. Debbie resisted, explaining that Sam could hear. Yes, the teacher said, but he needed to be able to communicate with the world. That made sense to Debbie. She wondered how she could have been so naive: she had assumed that one day Sam would simply start to speak. Until now, she had been used to his pointing at things he wanted. The first word he learned was "more," and soon he was telling his parents he wanted "more" of everything: more bottle, more outside, more hug, more food. His vocabulary developed swiftly. He learned how to sign his name, and Debbie's and David's, words for colors, and the information that he wanted to go to bed. One day he looked out a window and signed that Grandma's blue car was in front of the house.

At Sam's second-birthday party, one of the guests was a boy with severe cerebral palsy who had been with Sam at the hospital when he was born. The child was unresponsive. When his mother wasn't holding him, he lay on the carpet motionless, his eyes rolling involuntarily back and forth. It came time for Sam to blow out the candles on his cake, and his parents did it for him, as he couldn't control his breath. Yet they realized they had to some extent been blessed. Their son had a strange face, his ability to breathe was compromised, but his personality and spirit were intact. The Lightners, unlike the parents of the child with cerebral palsy, could connect with their son.

There were, of course, other problems. Sam's head was so big and heavy that he couldn't walk. He was able to sit, but the moment he tried to stand he fell over. A physical therapist worked with him, and when he was three he took his first steps. At four, he began speaking.

Even though Dr. Campbell had told the Lightners there was nothing he could do, they held out hope that surgeons would one day be able to remove the growth from Sam's face. When he was four, they consulted a surgeon who specialized in the ears, nose, and throat. He was optimistic, and suggested he start by removing tissue behind Sam's ear.

Immediately after removing only a small amount of tissue, the surgeon realized this was much tougher than he had thought. Sam bled heavily as the doctor sliced through the mass of vessels, and he was forced to close.

Even then, the incisions wouldn't heal. Sam bled uncontrollably, and needed blood transfusions. He was so thin that it took twelve attempts for nurses to locate a vein that could take the needle. David was mad at himself for having allowed the surgery. In his heart, he had known it was wrong. Never again, he vowed, would he authorize surgery on his son.

No matter what the doctors and nurses did, Sam's bleeding

wouldn't stop. He had been discharged from the hospital, and every day for weeks Debbie would have to take him back to have his dressing changed. When pulled away, the bandages would be soaked with blood. The surgeon opened Sam up a second time, trying to cauterize the blood vessels. But to no avail. Slowly, Sam was bleeding to death.

The surgeon told the Lightners he had no answer. The only hope was a powerful drug that would cause Sam's blood to coagulate. But with this there was the risk of a stroke. The surgeon did not want to tell the Lightners what to do; he wrote out a prescription and told them it was their choice.

That night, David Lightner prayed. "With all that we've been through, Lord," he said, "please don't let us lose this boy now."

Three days later, without the drug, Sam's bleeding stopped. The Lightners decided they would approve no additional surgeries—unless medically necessary—until their son was old enough to help guide the choice.

Debbie enrolled him in a school for medically fragile children. She was thrilled that he was making his way in the world, but distressed to learn that every other child in class was nonverbal. Sam ended up talking with the teachers. She and David felt that it was important for him to be around children from the neighborhood school. When Sam turned five, she went to enroll him at the local public kindergarten. Other parents and children waiting in line stared at him.

"This is Sam," Debbie said once she had filled out the necessary forms. "He's going to go to school here."

The teachers were leery. "Does he have mental problems?" one asked.

"No."

"Can he keep up?"

"Yes."

The principal was unsure. "Well . . ."

Debbie handed over the forms. "He *is* going to school here."

Once he was in school, Sam received extra attention daily from a speech therapist who helped him build strength in his voice. He mastered using his tongue and airflow to articulate words.

The school office staff, expecting a set of parents who would be always advocating for their special-needs child, were surprised that the Lightners never requested anything from the school. And this was true also after kindergarten. His parents never bailed Sam out, never let him use his condition as an excuse. A late or poorly done homework assignment, or being tardy for class, had nothing to do with his face. Debbie and David never asked a teacher to go easy on their son.

He grew into a good, and innovative, student. When the assignment was to report on any subject of the students' choosing, Sam prepared an exhaustive, thirty-five-page report on doughnuts. He researched how they were made, compared the taste of various doughnut stores' products, and provided a map pinpointing doughnut stores near the school. Not only did he receive an A on the report, but a clerk at one doughnut shop was so taken by Sam's resourcefulness that she gave him a free treat every time she saw him. He often found an excuse to wander past the shop, and sometimes came home with a bag full of doughnuts for his parents and younger sister and brother.

Sam didn't just work for good grades and then spend time alone in the library. In both grade school and middle school, he made friends with some of the most popular boys in his class. His best friend was athletic, involved in soccer, swimming, and track. He liked Sam's sense of humor, his ability to tease and play practical jokes. Sam never backed down. He would challenge this friend to a game of basketball—no running, just shooting at the hoop—and sometimes Sam would win. He developed a terrific shot from the foul line.

Sam played on the T-ball team, joined the Cub Scouts, and graduated to the Boy Scouts. A member of the Frog Patrol, he made the Tenderfoot rank, and worked on earning more merit badges. He tried basketball, but his head was so heavy that he fell easily. Swimming was impossible: the water would have poured in through the hole in his throat and made him drown.

No matter where he went, Sam attracted attention. Once when he and his friends were at a shopping mall, an older man asked Sam to bless him. The boys walked away, but the man followed, reaching for Sam's hand and again asking to be blessed. Sam finally turned to the man. "Bless you," he said, and then walked away laughing with his friends.

But at age eleven, something changed in Sam. He didn't laugh as much as before. Like many children at that age, he was self-conscious about his changing body. His friends could hide their insecurities behind clothes or new hairstyles. Sam couldn't alter the most prominent thing about himself—his face. When he was younger, Sam sensed that people felt sorry for him, but they didn't turn away from him. He'd never thought of his face as a burden. Yet now he sensed that people who saw his face for the first time assumed negative things about him. Sam never felt sorry for himself. But it was tedious to have to prove to people, again and again, that behind that mask he was just a normal boy.

At gatherings, he would sit with the adults, ignoring his parents' requests that he play with other children. When he encountered crowds, he turned his head to one side. When he walked with his parents in public, he would look for the nearest wall and walk next to it so people wouldn't see the left side of his face. Or he'd stand behind his parents, so they would block the view.

The younger Sam had never done things like these. He was always the one to lead the family into stores, movie theaters, restaurants. Debbie and David asked him what was wrong. He wanted to look normal, he told them. The issue that his parents thought was resolved—surgery—came back into play. They told Sam that the risks worried them, that they couldn't forget what had happened when he was four, and how the uncontrollable bleeding had scared them. Sam replied that he wanted his face fixed. He wasn't seeking perfection, he simply wanted to look more normal.

His parents were ambivalent. They loved their son just as he was. He knew that their love was true and real. But as he grew older, the world outside, with all its requirements and expectations and prejudices, called to him.

Debbie and David considered Sam's future, his education and eventual employment. Would people discriminate against him? People saw him and assumed so many things were wrong with him. A lot of Sam's friends had girlfriends. Sam had never even danced with a girl. Was it because he was shy, or were girls afraid of him? Sam's parents didn't want the world to be scared of their son. And the reality of the world, the Lightners knew, was that people judged others by the way they looked. They didn't want Sam to come to them when he was thirty and ask why they hadn't tried to help him when he was a child. If Sam was ready for surgery, then they would have to be too. This was, after all, what they had resolved when he was four.

They went looking for another surgeon, and found an ear, nose, and throat specialist at Oregon Health & Science University. Sam was thrilled, and couldn't wait to meet with him. After examining Sam, the doctor was blunt: If the boy had an operation to remove the mass, he would die. Sam left the appointment in tears. Never again would he let himself get his hopes up.

His parents continued to look. After six months, a surgeon who chaired the university's Department of Plastic and Reconstructive Surgery agreed to examine Sam. Like the previous surgeon, he understood that a procedure might destroy vital nerves and blood vessels, leaving Sam with a paralyzed face, if not doing more damage. Hundreds of vessels ran through the deformed tissue, and any incision would cause terrible bleeding. He could bleed to death on the operating table. The Lightners had a tough choice. From talking with him, the surgeon knew that Sam's deformity had not interfered with his personality. He was smart, and mature beyond his years. If Sam were his son, he'd make sure the boy understood the medical problems involved. Then, if he still wanted to undergo surgery, his wishes should be honored.

Sam did not change his mind.

The surgery was scheduled for June 1998, just after the school year ended. A week before the operation was to take place, the surgeon and his partner peered down Sam's throat, to study the mass without having to make an incision. They didn't like what they saw. That afternoon, the surgeon met with the Lightners. He had made an agonizing decision: The surgery was too risky. In good faith, he could not operate.

The news devastated Sam. He had maintained some hope that a surgeon would be able to help him. Now he was trapped, destined to live the rest of his life with this deformation.

He would make the best of it.

That fall, when Sam was thirteen, the Lightners were invited to a Halloween birthday party that Debbie's friend Mary was throwing for her husband. More than seventy people attended the costume party. Debbie and David Lightner went as outlaw bikers. Sam put orange coloring in his hair and a gel to make it stick straight up. He wandered through Mary's house, among grown men in cheerleader miniskirts and wigs, and diminutive witches, ghosts, and goblins. He picked at food from the buffet in the dining room, then went to find something to drink. Mary told him the drinks were on the back porch. He took a can of pop from a cooler there and returned to the kitchen, where Mary was preparing more food. A woman came into the kitchen to tell Mary how wonderful the party was. The woman nodded at Sam.

"Look at that mask," she said.

Sam didn't move. He looked at the floor, hoping the woman would leave. But she didn't. She tapped Mary on the shoulder and pointed at Sam.

"That's a great mask," she said.

Mary leaned toward the woman. "It's not a mask."

The woman laughed. "No way," she said loudly. "Something that good has to be a mask."

She walked over to Sam. His eyes met hers.

"Oh my God!" she said.

Sam slipped out of the kitchen. He found comfort in the dark living room, where people could pretend.

5   Sam pedaled as hard as he could, but he could not keep up with his family. His legs ached, and he panted for breath. Even his little brother could bicycle farther, longer, faster. Most of the time during this spring vacation in March 1999, Sam wanted to lie in bed and watch television.

When he spoke, people kept asking him to repeat himself. No one—not the desk clerk at the lodge in central Oregon where the Lightners were staying; not the woman in the gift shop; not even his family—could understand him. His speech was garbled, as if his mouth were full of food. But he wasn't eating. Breakfast, lunch, and dinner, he would sit and barely touch his food, wanting only to go lie down.

"Come here, Sam," his mother said one morning when they were back at home. "I want to weigh you."

Over his protests, she took him to the bathroom.

"Five pounds," she said. "You've lost five pounds."

She scheduled an appointment with his pediatrician. Although he determined nothing specifically wrong, the pediatrician, Dr. Steve Davis, was concerned about the weight loss—Sam was already too thin—and thought the boy might be anemic. He prescribed iron pills, and laughingly told Sam to eat more.

But Sam continued to lose weight.

One morning he woke up in pain, touched his face and found it tender. The mass was growing. Debbie gave him Advil, but the mass continued to swell. Within a week, Sam was unable to swallow the pill. His tongue felt bigger. He started crying continually. A specialist examined a lump that had suddenly appeared on his shoulder and wrote a prescription for Tylenol with codeine. That helped reduce the pain for about a week. When school let out in June, Sam was in constant pain.

The family decided to go ahead with a vacation they had planned. Before leaving, Sam went to a doctor, who found nothing wrong, but gave the Lightners a prescription for a strong painkiller just in case. When they returned from vacation, Sam could no longer swallow even soft food. He had to drink liquid protein, and his weight continued to drop as the pain increased. In July, the specialist again examined the lump on his shoulder. Believing it had grown and could be pressing on a nerve, he decided to remove it.

Sam was in and out of the hospital in one day. There were no complications, but the pain lingered, and had spread into his neck and around his face.

One day in early August, Sam came downstairs from his bedroom. He found his mother on the front porch. He went to sit next to her, crying. His speech was slurred, and he had to repeat himself.

The pain, he managed to tell her, had spread across the entire left side of his face.

The next morning his mother took him to Emanuel Hospital. Nurses and doctors poked and probed. He sat still while strange machines whirled around him. And then he waited while specialists reviewed the X rays and CAT scans. They found nothing. Sam refused to go home. Someone, he pleaded, had to help him. Doctors admitted him and ran more tests. Four days later, the mass awakened.

Pain racked Sam's body. He tried to call for help but couldn't speak. His swollen tongue stuck several inches out of his mouth. He reached for the button beside his pillow to call for help.

He wrote in a notebook to communicate with nurses and doctors:

*I have no idea why. Since I was a baby. I was born with this.*
*Don't touch.*
*Please, it hurts.*
*Extra morphine. I want nurse Sara. In pain. Want extra morphine.*
He held out his arm so nurses could give him morphine.

No one knew what to do to help the boy. He was being fed through a tube that ran into his stomach, and was being given antibiotics, as if he had an infection. Nothing helped. A nurse told Sam's parents they should bring a poster to his room. Their son would be in the hospital for some time, and it would be comforting to him if his room was personalized.

He wrote his mother a note:

*I officially weigh 65.6 lbs. They don't have smaller gowns.*
*When will I be able to talk and eat? I want something to taste.*
Each day things got a little worse.
*My hand is cold. They need to find out what this is.*
One day when Debbie came to sit with him, Sam scribbled out this message in his notebook:

*If I had had the surgery would this be happening to me?*

Debbie Lightner thought for a moment.

"I don't know," she told him.

One afternoon, Dr. Tim Campbell came to Emanuel's Pediatric School-Age Unit, where a patient was recovering. Having seen that his patient was doing well, Campbell went to the nurses' station to talk. He glanced at the board that listed patients' names and room numbers, and saw a name that seemed familiar.

*Sam Lightner.*

Campbell tried to remember where he'd heard the name before. And then it hit him—the little boy he had operated on almost fourteen years earlier. He hadn't seen the boy since then. Campbell had a few minutes to spare, so he thought he'd pay a visit. He walked down the hall and stopped in front of Sam's room, and opened the pull-down box hanging on the wall by the door, where patients' charts were held for medical staff. Campbell wondered why Sam was here. He scanned the report. The boy weighed sixty-five pounds—he was wasting away. Campbell pushed open the door to Sam's room.

The boy lay motionless in bed, his bloated face spilled across most of the pillow. His tongue protruded from his mouth, and the swelling on the left side of his face wrenched one eye completely out of position. The deformity he'd carried since birth was now a life-threatening size, choking off his airway and esophagus.

Sam, Campbell thought, was giving up—in medical slang, "circling the drain." Campbell had seen this look in children battling terminal cancer. At a certain time, they accepted their fate and surrendered to death.

"Do you know who I am?" Campbell asked.

Sam's eyes flickered. He shook his head.

"I'm Dr. Tim Campbell."

The name meant nothing to Sam. Just another doctor.

"I operated on you a long time ago," Campbell said.

Sam didn't respond.

"How do you feel?"

Sam struggled to sit up. He reached for his notebook to reply.

*Anything to stop the headaches. When I cough hard, little capillaries burst and blood comes out.*

The boy was being killed from within.

Sam scribbled another note.

*I really don't think this is going to work out.*

Campbell sought to reassure him. "The doctors are trying."

*Please try your hardest.*

"Hang in there, Sambo."

*I'm in pain. It was really bad this morning.*

Campbell made a note to order more morphine.

*I hurt.*

And methadone.

"Try to sleep."

*Will it kill me?*

Campbell didn't have an answer.

He was haunted by what he'd seen. He could hardly imagine what this boy's life had been like for the last fourteen years. Someone had to help him. Surgery was out: there was no way to operate without putting the boy's life at risk. The mass remained a mystery. New research postulated that such masses were like benign tumors, growing like cancers. But no one knew for sure where they came from, how they grew, or how to eliminate them.

Campbell went to the nurses' station and called the hospital's tumor board. The group, made up of medical specialists, met twice a month to discuss treatment of children with tumors. Campbell, by now a hospital veteran, thought that doctors who had come to

Emanuel from elsewhere in the country might have encountered something like Sam's condition during their training.

When he returned to Sam's room, Campbell found Debbie and reintroduced himself. He told her that he had Sam's case scheduled for discussion by the tumor specialists. But, he said, "I want to do something different, if it's okay with you and Sam."

He pulled up a chair and sat beside the bed.

"I want to do something I've never done in all the years I've been meeting with these doctors," he said. "I want them to see the patient."

He leaned over and looked at Sam. "I want them to see you."

He turned to Debbie. "I want other people to look at him and appreciate the problem."

To get to the meeting, Sam would have to be pushed through the hospital in a wheelchair. Campbell knew that people would be gawking at him.

"Is that okay?" Campbell asked. Debbie nodded. Sam answered in the notebook.

*Yes.*

Campbell took Debbie aside. "He'll be in there just a short time," he promised. "Sixty seconds. I'll make sure that he doesn't feel like he's on display."

At the next meeting of the tumor board, after everyone was seated, Campbell spoke. "There's a child three floors up in this hospital who's in bad shape," he said. "He needs help, whatever help we can give him."

The reaction around the room was what he expected. Every child in the hospital needed help.

"I don't know what to do," Campbell admitted. "But something has to happen, or this boy will die."

He outlined his history with Sam, the surgery when the boy was just born and how he hadn't been able to help then. Now that he had come upon Sam again, he knew he had to help. The board members had Sam's records, including X rays, in front of them.

"I'm looking for ideas on how to help him. Any ideas."

As the doctors looked through the papers before them, Campbell motioned to a secretary. The door opened and an attendant wheeled Sam Lightner into the room. He was slumped in the chair. The short trip to the conference room had been hard on him, but Campbell was proud of him for coming.

The doctors looked up at the visitor, aghast at the sight. That was the reaction Campbell wanted. They had to see the magnitude of the problem, the mass itself and the despair in the boy's face. Words alone could not convey Sam's condition. After a minute, Campbell motioned to the attendant to take Sam back to his room. When the door closed behind them, Campbell turned to his colleagues.

"Now what?" he asked.

There was a pause.

"There must be something that can be done," Campbell insisted.

The other doctors agreed with what others had already determined. Surgery was out, they were certain.

"Tim," one doctor said, "there's really nothing we can tell you. We can't help this boy."

The board turned its attention to the next case.

**6** Campbell couldn't get Sam Lightner out of his mind. It was impossible to ignore this case. One day he came across a newspaper article about the cancer researcher Judah Folkman, whom Campbell had met thirty years earlier when they were both young surgeons.

Folkman worked at Boston Children's Hospital and headed a team of researchers who had succeeded in controlling tumors in mice with anti-angiogenesis drugs—drugs that stifle the growth of the blood vessels supplying those tumors. Campbell considered the fact that a wild excess of blood vessels had created Sam's deformity. Maybe Folkman's method could work on the boy. He found Folkman's telephone number in a doctors' directory and placed the call.

After some small talk, Campbell got to the point. He explained

Sam's malformation and his deteriorating condition, both physical and emotional, and told Folkman of the tumor board's decision. What to do? Might Folkman's procedure work on the boy?

Folkman's response was discouraging. Sam's malformation was fully formed, and his method worked only on growing tumors. He suggested that Campbell call Jennifer Marler, a pediatric surgeon who had worked for him as a research fellow and was now a member of the Children's Hospital Vascular Anomalies Team, which treated malformations like Sam's.

Campbell did so, and Marler told him to send her the boy's medical file along with photographs of him. She could take a look, but she wasn't promising anything.

Campbell told the Lightners that he had spoken to Marler, and he obtained their consent to take some pictures and send Sam's file.

Then the doctor went to see Sam in the hospital. The boy stared straight into the camera while Campbell photographed him.

"This is for a doctor in Boston," Campbell said.

Sam was again realizing how much he hated being in the hospital. He missed his home, his friends. He was tired of the constant pain. For the first time in his life, he was starting to feel sorry for himself—not because of the way he looked, but because this condition was making it impossible to live, to be out in the world.

The IV line in his arm pumped him full of drugs: morphine, methadone, Celebrex, and nortriptyline—painkillers, anti-inflammatories, antidepressants. One day a doctor Sam had not met before, a psychiatrist, showed up at his bedside.

The doctor explained that hospital social workers were concerned about Sam's emotional state. He'd spoken with Sam's parents, and they agreed to let a professional talk with him. The doctor began asking questions, which Sam answered in his notebook. Then he asked a question.

*Why is this happening?*

Sam wasn't asking for sympathy, wasn't complaining. He wanted a medical answer.

*Why am I in such pain?*

The psychiatrist had no answer. He changed the subject: "Tell me how you feel about life. Is life unfair?"

So many thoughts rushed through Sam's mind: How stupid. My tongue is sticking three inches out of my mouth. I can't eat. My left eye bulges out of its socket, and the pressure of this thing is growing every hour. No one knows how to get rid of it. He considered the question: Is life unfair?

*Sometimes.*

In the next few days, just as unpredictably as it had begun, the swelling receded. And just as they couldn't explain why it had erupted, the doctors couldn't explain why it was abating. On September 2, 1999, after some three weeks in the hospital, Sam reluctantly went home.

Yes, he had wanted to go home. But now he was apprehensive. He was afraid the pain would return. The nurses assured him that they'd send him home with all the medication he would need.

Sam had lost seventeen pounds since early August; he now weighted sixty-three. He couldn't speak. He was listless, did not stir from his bed. One day he motioned his mother over. He held out his notebook.

*I'm worried about missing school.*

His mother told him not to worry. She arranged for a tutor to come to the house so that Sam wouldn't fall behind.

In November, Sam went back to school for the first time this autumn. He seemed to have resigned himself to his fate. He would go to the lunchroom with his classmates, but then quietly disappear to the nurse's office. There he would pour nutritional formula into the tube that led directly to his stomach. He felt like a baby. And the only thing anyone at school talked about now was high school, next year.

7  The Vascular Anomalies Team at Boston Children's Hospital had its humble beginnings in the late 1970s, when surgeon and medical researcher John Mulliken grew curious about cases he was encountering in the hospital's pediatric plastic surgery clinic.

The medical literature he turned to could not adequately explain the phenomenon. The defects he saw in these children were rare enough, and Mulliken began compiling data, taking photographs, examining in the lab, and writing case studies. The database, at first nothing more than sheets in a binder, expanded until Mulliken had to enter it into the computer.

Mulliken is now credited as the father of the field that he named "vascular anomalies." A cofounder of the International Society for the Study of Vascular Anomalies, he lectures around the world. He has written some 185 scientific articles, forty book chapters, and two complete books.

The headquarters was a small windowless office at the end of a hallway. Nevertheless people from all over found it, in one way or another. A doctor in Des Moines might see a vascular malformation for the first time in his career and wouldn't know what to tell the parents, aside from what to call it. They would get on the Internet, type in the word "hemangioma," and learn about Mulliken and his team. And so they would write him, asking for help. Or they would prod the doctor to contact Mulliken to see if he had any suggestions.

The team's coordinator received an average of sixty-five inquiries from parents and doctors daily. The envelopes and packages, which arrived from around the world, were opened, and the contents—pictures, medical reports, charts—were placed in folders, each of which told a story of fear and hopelessness:

"She is 15 . . . and her right forearm has a severe malformation. Two resections were performed but we need help."

"He bumped his head on the ceramic tile of the kitchen floor while throwing a temper tantrum. Initially he did not appear to have any complications as a result. . . . Until that time in his life, he was an overall healthy child."

"We have tried everything. He is suffering terribly and it is time to consider letting him go. All of these are impossible decisions [for] a parent of this precious little boy with so much life to live. That is where you come in."

"If you have any thoughts or suggestions on the avenues to pursue from our bleak list of choices, we would be grateful for the input. If you have any information that might improve his life, even temporarily, we would request an immediate response from you. His condition is very rare. But by studying our little boy, you might help to save another."

Dr. Jennifer Marler, a junior surgeon and research fellow on the Vascular Anomalies Team, spent little time in her office. Most of the workday she shuttled between her lab and the operating room.

At the end of this September day, after a brutal round of surgeries and clinics, Marler returned to her office for her jacket and purse. She was about to switch off the light and head home to her husband and children when she spotted a packet on her chair. She picked it up and read the sender's name in the corner: Dr. Tim Campbell.

It didn't register with Marler, but she knew that if she didn't deal with the packet now, it would get lost or forgotten in the paperwork constantly piling up on her desk.

She opened the packet and turned it upside down, dropping the contents onto her desk. She picked up a medical report. "Patient has lymphaticovenous malformation of the left side of face and neck. Condition was diagnosed prenatally. Involvement of the airway necessitated a tracheotomy. Difficulty swallowing necessitated a gastronomy tube. Malformation has grown to the point of orbital dystopia. . . . The boy was having intractable pain and unable to eat. He was on a morphine drip and diagnosed as clinically depressed."

Now she remembered: the Portland boy, Campbell had called her about him.

She looked through the photos of the boy, stopping at what seemed to be the most recent. In the course of her work, in this country and abroad, Marler had seen children who had lost all hope. This boy in a hospital bed stared at the camera with pleading eyes that reminded her of those desperate, terribly sad-looking kids. She saw no life in his eyes. She was reminded of a man in his sixties who was only now being treated for a malformation that had taken over his face, making him look like something out of a horror movie. Marler had tracked him down—he lived outside a small town, a recluse. She didn't want this Portland boy to have to hide from the world like that.

Marler now looked for the earliest photo, taken apparently at birth. She turned the picture horizontally and examined the mass on the left side of the baby's face.

Having cleared a space on her desk, she placed the two pictures side by side. With a ruler she measured the distance between the nose and the left cheek in each picture. The distance in the later picture was smaller than in the earlier one. As rudimentary as the measure was, it told Marler that the mass had grown faster than the boy's body.

She looked at the first photograph again: The left eye was normal. In the later picture, the eye was grossly distorted, pushed out of place, seemingly useless, because the mass had expanded. The mass was growing, it was alive, it might kill the boy. As Marler saw it, this boy should have an operation.

Operating on a vascular anomaly was tricky, she was aware, and operating on one this complex was beyond her ability. But the Vascular Anomalies Team could help the boy.

Among the photographs on Marler's office wall were those of children who had set the course of her life. Some were children she had operated on successfully, relieving them of deformities that would have robbed them of a future. Others, however, were children who had died from their abnormalities or who didn't survive risky surgery intended to help them.

She looked at the picture of the boy again. He had given up. But to her he was too young to have no hope.

Marler hoped that eventually kids like this wouldn't need surgery. That's why she spent so much of her time in the lab. She believed the answer to malformations was in the test tube, in the anti-angiogenesis drugs.

She would try to see this Sam Lightner. Examining him might give her useful information for the lab and eventually help other children. But more pressing, she wanted to help him in the operating room. Everyone else deemed surgery too risky, and that was understandable. It would be difficult, and Marler had to admit that she had never seen a patient with a craniofacial malformation as bad as Sam's. Yet she could not refuse this boy. She telephoned the team scheduler and asked to present Sam's case and argue that he be brought to Boston.

The Vascular Anomalies Team met every Wednesday evening in the hospital's surgical library. Members of the team and associated fellows and residents gathered around a table, discussing cases, viewing slides of patients, exchanging information, posing questions. Pagers went off repeatedly, and doctors wandered in and out of the library to take calls.

In their conversations, the doctors were not hesitant to challenge one another, pointing out problems that might rule out surgery. Marler studied the sheet in front of her. Nineteen children were up for consideration. Maybe not even half would be chosen. The team moved quickly down the list, deciding yes for an eight-month-old girl from Argentina, a three-year-old girl from Italy, a nine-year-old boy from Minnesota.

Sam Lightner was next. Marler pushed the button for the slide projector. Sam's picture, one Dr. Campbell had taken at the hospital in Portland, flashed on the screen.

Marler spoke deliberately. She wanted the team to know something of the boy's life. She gave them details that Campbell had written her.

"He's in pain," she concluded. "Without hope."

She was aware that Sam's case presented major problems. He had already had two surgeries when he was younger. Scar tissue would make things difficult, and the other doctors zeroed in on the risks.

"There's nothing we can do," one of them said.

Next case.

Marler scheduled Sam for the November meeting. Again the answer was no.

As she waited to enter the library for the next meeting, Marler knew this was the end. There was no way she could present this case a fourth time. That would only irritate the other doctors. She had plotted a strategy. This was her last chance. And Sam's.

She would focus not on the entire team, but on one man—John Mulliken. There were only a handful of surgeons in the United States who could perform the complicated cases Mulliken handled with ease. But she was convinced that he was the only one who could take on Sam's case. Mulliken was the last to enter, and he took a seat at the end of the table. Marler moved to sit next to him.

His credentials notwithstanding, Marler's choice of Mulliken as a partner was curious: they made for an unlikely alliance. He was single, in his sixties, a world-renowned plastic surgeon and researcher. He lived in Brookline, an affluent suburb ten minutes from the hospital, and traced his roots to a wealthy colonial family. Marler considered Mulliken a genius, but one infuriatingly isolated from the real world. He rarely took vacations, and could be found in the operating room, his lab, or his office well into the night and on weekends.

Marler, although she had been a doctor for eleven years, was still finding her way in the medical world. She was the daughter of an immigrant medical technician, married with three children—and struggling.

Mulliken tried to relate with patients, but often fell short. Worried parents would tell him how they felt. He'd reply, in all seriousness, that he understood, that he had a dog and a cat he loved. A cabinet in his operating room carried nineteen photographs of Girlie and Felicia. If Marler had a chance to speak with the parents, she would run interference for the older doctor.

She and Mulliken were similar, however, in two things: both were fascinated by how things worked, and both were self-described vascular nuts. Tonight, Marler had to find a way to capitalize on those common interests, and make Mulliken understand Sam's desperation, and the fear facing his family.

It wouldn't be easy.

The meeting started. Marler stood and outlined the Sam Lightner case yet again. She saw the quizzical looks of her colleagues. This was a case they had already rejected as too risky, why were they reviewing it once more? The doctors didn't even bother referring to the paperwork.

"We all know this boy's story," Marler said. "And we've already heard that there's nothing that can be done, that can help him.

"If he were my child and no one would agree to operate, what would I do?" she asked. "I'd do whatever I could to persuade someone. I think we need to help him."

The other doctors looked at Mulliken. It was his call. He would be the surgeon.

She studied Mulliken, an impatient man, as he reviewed the report on Sam. He couldn't ignore the likelihood of nerve damage and the possibility of horrendous, even fatal bleeding.

"John," she said, "no one else will operate."

Mulliken was reluctant. There was no way he could get the mass of tissue out and make Sam's face symmetrical.

She appealed to his pride. "They say it can't be done."

She appealed to his compassion. "If our team is going to serve anyone, it is a kid like this," Marler said. "We have to help him."

She kept staring at Mulliken, until he looked her in the eye.

"You're his last hope," she told him.

Maybe it was her youthful enthusiasm. Maybe he was reminded of being a junior surgeon in South Korea, visiting leper colonies and orphanages to operate on children with facial deformities so severe that village elders thought it best the children be left to die. Sam was like one of those lepers, shunned by the world because of his face.

Mulliken slapped the table in front of him.

"Bring him to Boston," he growled.

8   Jennifer Marler stopped in her office and dug out the Lightner file. She found the phone number she wanted on a form—the bank where Debbie Lightner worked as a teller. Marler called and asked for Debbie; it wasn't a direct line, and she had to wait a minute or two.

"Hi, this is Debbie Lightner. Thanks for holding."

"Hello, this is Dr. Jennifer Marler, calling from Boston. Can you talk right now?"

"Just a minute." Debbie put the doctor on hold and went to the phone that tellers were to use for personal calls. She punched the button to pick up the line.

"I'm back."

"Let me start over," Marler said. "I'm Dr. Jennifer Marler, and I'm calling from Boston Children's Hospital."

Debbie was puzzled. She didn't recall ever talking to anyone in Boston, and she didn't remember any Dr. Marler.

"Your doctor"—she searched through her papers—"Tim Campbell contacted me. He wanted advice on your son's case. He sent me information on your son."

That was so long ago, Debbie thought. She assumed that Campbell's efforts had been fruitless.

"Okay," she said. "Now I remember."

"Good. I'm calling to let you know that I presented your son's case to the Vascular Anomalies Team."

"What's that?" Debbie looked up and saw the line of customers waiting to be served. She told the doctor that she had to get back to work.

"I'll call you at home tonight, around nine your time," Marler said. "Is that okay? For now I want you to know that the team reviewed your son's case. We think we can help."

Debbie stood up to show that she'd be back at her window momentarily. First, though, she had a question for Marler.

"How?"

"To start, we need to see him in person," Marler explained. "He needs to be evaluated. I'll tell you all about it tonight, but I wanted to give you the good news right away."

When the phone rang at the Lightners' that night, Debbie sat at the dining room table with the portable, hoping it would be quiet enough to talk. Marler explained the Vascular Anomalies Team to her, how these specialists exchanged information and experiences.

"Who'll evaluate Sam?" Debbie asked.

"Dr. John Mulliken heads the team," Marler said. But other people on the team would advise him.

Debbie reached for an envelope that was on the table, and a pencil on the hutch behind her. She asked Marler to spell Mulliken's name. She told Marler Sam's history, and recounted how every doctor in Oregon had backed away from surgery. Was this going to happen again? Why fly cross-country on a whim?

"There's no guarantee that Sam will be a candidate for surgery," Marler warned. "But getting him to Boston is a critical first step."

"We know there's no miracle out there," Debbie said. "We've learned not to get our hopes up. I guess we can be happy that someone's willing to assess his situation.

"Can you tell me about Dr. Mulliken?" Debbie asked.

"When it comes to vascular anomalies, he's the world's best. Let me put it this way: I have three children, and if any one of them needed a surgeon, I'd take them to John Mulliken. I promise you that your son will be well taken care of. But we'll need to see Sam in person first."

"Okay," Debbie said. "I'll talk with my husband and Sam. We'll let you know."

Debbie wasn't sure what to believe. She went to the computer, in the basement, hoping to find something about Mulliken on the Internet. When she typed in his name, there were four hits.

The first one told her about Mulliken's education, his academic appointments, and his current position as associate professor of surgery at Harvard Medical School. One thing especially caught Debbie's eye. Among the doctor's research projects was the "molecular basis for craniofacial and vascular malformations."

Maybe, she thought. Maybe this time.


For the next several months, the Lightners coolly evaluated the offer. They were in no rush to go to Boston. Sam was physically on the mend after the flare-up that had sent him to the hospital in

August. He was in school and doing well in his classes. A trip to the East Coast seemed disruptive.

But this was the news that Sam had been waiting for. Finally, a doctor who believed he might be able to help. Sam told his parents that he wanted to be evaluated by this team in Boston. He had given up hope that anyone could help, and now someone said there was a chance. That's all he wanted—just a chance.

That hope, his parents decided, was worth the cost of an airline ticket.

On April 6, 2000, Sam Lightner and his parents headed to the Portland airport. Sam had never been on a jet before, and he was excited simply being in the airport. He didn't care that people were staring at him—he was headed East to pursue a dream.

"Where are you going?" an attendant asked him at the gate.

"To a hospital in Boston," Sam said.

Her face softened. "I'll try to move you to first class if there's an empty seat."

"That's okay," Sam told her. "I'm with my parents, and they promised me the window seat."

The cab driver at the airport in Boston took one look at Sam and had to comment. Not about his face, but about his New York Yankees baseball cap.

"Not in this town, kid," he said with a laugh.

The Lightners were staying at a hotel two blocks from Boston Children's Hospital. They took the elevator to their floor and walked down a narrow hallway to their room. The hallway would have looked like one in any hotel, except for what stood in front of many of the doors. Not room service trays, but oxygen tanks, metal hospital cribs, and suction machines just like Sam's. The guests of this hotel hadn't come to Boston for fun. They were here because

they or someone they loved needed help from the doctors down the
street.

The next morning the Lightners went through the main entrance of Boston Children's, where children were welcomed in English and nine other languages. There were at least a dozen empty
wheelchairs out front. For once in his life, Sam didn't feel out of
place. He saw a child being pushed in a wheelchair, an oxygen mask
over his face. The child was a dwarf. Sam thought he looked like a
living doll. He saw a girl with no legs, whose parents had to carry
her out of a taxicab and lower her into a wheelchair. Here, no child
stared at another. Here, they were all different, and therefore all alike.

Sam followed his parents to the information counter. On it was
a white wicker basket full of pennies to be tossed into a nearby wishing well. Attached to the basket was a sign: "Help yourself to only
two, your first wish for me, the second for you. The wish for me
is you get better real soon, the one for yourself, the best of life's for-
tune. To all of you—quick healing and good health for all time. Be
strong!"

While his parents were orienting themselves, Sam plucked out
two pennies. He looked at them, closed his right eye, and tossed the
pennies into the well.

Eventually Sam and his parents made their way to the Vascular
Unit, which shared a waiting room with Pediatric Surgery on the
third floor. Children's toys littered the floor, and cartoons played on
a television set. Sam found a seat next to a window, and flipped
through a stack of magazines. He found publications for younger
kids, and for their parents. But nothing for a fourteen-year-old boy.

The waiting room began to fill. The kids here were serious
cases; a blind girl in a wheelchair, her limbs contorted; a boy with a
deformed leg, partially hidden under a blanket. As each patient ar-

rived, Sam saw how different his deformity was—not just in sever-ity, but also in location. When he looked at the boy with the bad leg, for instance, the leg seemed merely a part of the boy. But Sam's face was who he was. And when he looked at the other children's par-ents, they seemed to him to be telling themselves that no matter what was wrong with their child, at least that child did not have a face like that boy across the waiting room.

One woman stared at Sam when he wasn't looking, then whis-pered to a woman sitting next to her, and finally gave up all pretense and watched Sam, mesmerized.

His left eye looked bad today, puffy and barely open, as if he had been punched. His left ear was the color of eggplant. And with each breath he wheezed, his tongue sticking out of a distorted mouth that he could not close. Sam saw the woman watching, and turned away. Minutes later he heard the receptionist call his name.

In the examination room, Sam climbed onto the table.

"You've been waiting for this for a long time," his mother said.

Sam nodded.

"Do you have any questions for the doctor?"

He shrugged.

9   There was a soft knock on the door to the examination room, and a woman in a white doctor's smock entered. "I'm Dr. Marler," she said. She shook hands with Debbie and David, then turned her attention to Sam.

Everything she'd thought about him after seeing his pictures was true. He was a real textbook case. She was aware too that surgery wasn't a cure for him. Any kind of surgery was going to be tough. Sam was the kind of kid she wanted to develop therapies for in the lab.

"I'm so glad to meet you," she told Sam. A flush spread up his neck. This woman was pretty. And kind. He hoped she could help him.

The Lightners explained Sam's medical history—the emergency surgery right after birth, the ear surgery that led to six weeks of persistent bleeding, and again, the reluctance of other surgeons to attempt cutting away the main mass of tissue.

"This was present at birth?" Marler asked. "Was it diagnosed prenatally?" Marler took notes as both Debbie and David described Sam's life till now, and showed her photos of him at various ages.

"Last summer was the climax," David said. "It was the worst it had ever been. And that happened after a doctor backed out at the last minute, five days before Sam was scheduled for surgery."

Marler shook her head. "That's rough. But I think you're in the right place now. We see a lot of kids with these kinds of problems. Dr. Mulliken is both a craniofacial surgeon and a specialist in vascular anomalies. That makes him the right man for the job."

She turned to face the examination table. "So let's take a look, Sam." She patted his knee. He smiled.

"What grade are you in?"

"Eighth," he said, in his raspy voice.

"Are you still having pain?"

"No."

"It is totally gone?"

"Yes."

"No problems, none whatsoever?"

"No."

Marler ran her fingers across the mass. She sighed. This was a bad one. Mulliken might just walk away from this.

She tried to think like Mulliken, looking for the weaknesses in the case before he found them, the arguments to set forth so he would have to agree to surgery.

"Look up for me," she told Sam. "Open your mouth wide, wide, wide. . . . Smile. . . . Can you bring your teeth together? . . . Just on that one side of your mouth?"

She was jotting notes to herself, Sam saw, and he wondered what she was writing. Was she still going to try to help him?

"Now look up again for me. How is your vision, Sam? Is it pretty good?"

He nodded.

"He used to be able to see much better," David said. "But all he can see out of his left eye now is shapes and darkness."

"If I understand it," Marler said, "your goal is to try to debulk his face and make it look cosmetically better."

Sam let his parents answer for him.

"Yes," Debbie said. "And maybe you can relieve some of the pressure on his eye. At one time it was the size of a golf ball."

David cleared his throat. "He's going into the ninth grade. He's more concerned about his appearance now. He'd like his head made smaller."

"I can understand that, Sam," Marler said. "I'll bring in Dr. Mulliken and our cast of thousands. On this one, we're going to need everyone's expert opinion."

She excused herself, and said she would be back soon.

"Nervous?" David asked his son.

"I'm just hoping, Dad."

When Marler returned, she was accompanied by six other people in doctor's smocks, who formed a semicircle around Sam. One of them, who was wearing a bow tie with blue and red polkadots, stepped forward.

"Hi, Sam. I'm Dr. Mulliken. Nice to meet you."

He took the boy's head in his hands and ran his fingers over it gently. He frowned. The blue veins showing through Sam's waxen skin worried him.

What always moved Mulliken were the faces of children who

found their way to the third floor of Boston Children's Hospital. He had come to discover another side of living with a facial deformity: it wasn't about science or medicine, it was about emotions and about being shunned.

Mulliken looked at Sam's face. The doctor in him saw a big, slow-flow malformation, the massive overgrowth on the left side. The man in him, the man who had listened to hundreds of parents, saw a boy carrying a terrible burden. He had to be honest, with himself and this family.

"Oh, my," he finally said. "There's a lot of venous component here. This is an incredible overgrowth."

He released Sam's head and stepped back, crossing his arms. He looked like a sculptor studying a block of granite.

"I don't think I've ever seen an ear like this. I've certainly seen big ears with malformations. But the skin has separated from the cartilage."

Marler could imagine what Mulliken was thinking: This was going to be—at best—a difficult case. Would he hurt this boy, or would he help him?

The size of a mass and its location were just two problems. The operations Sam had had as a baby had left scar tissue that would be hellish when Mulliken needed to find facial nerves to avoid. There was no question that surgery would be difficult. There was no way to predict what would happen. Mulliken could walk away now, leave this examination room; he had nothing to prove. Jennifer Marler, though, believed she had everything to prove.

Marler knew it was time for her to sell Mulliken on doing the surgery. "I'm impressed by how much is soft tissue," she said.

"There's a lot of soft tissue on the floor of the mouth, but this is bone," Mulliken replied. "This is all bone."

"I think he has very good facial nerve function," Marler countered.

"Smile, Sam," Mulliken commanded.

"Marginal over here," he said. "The distortion of the lower jaw is out of sorts from what I would expect in a lymphatic malformation. What incredible overgrowth."

He touched Sam's left eyelid. "How is the eye doing? Does it get swollen very often?"

"Not that often," Sam said.

The room was silent. Everyone looked at Mulliken. Sam didn't know if he should move.

"Do we have any plain films?"

"No," Marler said.

"How about a panorex?"

"No."

"Let's get that," Mulliken said. "I don't have a lot of feeling for the bone underneath. What's the baseline under all this?"

He turned to the Lightners. "How long are you going to be around?"

"We go home in two days," Debbie said.

Mulliken sighed. "Okay, let's write down some things."

That was what Marler had been waiting to hear. He was definitely going to take the case. She smiled and opened her notebook, ready to record what Mulliken needed to know about the inside of Sam Lightner's head.

"I want Reza to look down the trach and see what's going on there," Mulliken said, asking that one of his colleagues examine Sam's airway. "Send him to AP for a panorex. Find a CP and get pictures downstairs. We're going to have to decide what's going on in terms of flow, and if there's anything we can do to make it easier." He looked at Marler. "Got all that?"

"Right," she said.

Mulliken scooted next to Sam as if he were his grandfather. He put his hand on the boy's knee.

"What bothers you the most?" he asked. "If you could have one thing you wanted, what would that be?"

Sam shrugged. He had waited so long for a doctor to say he could help that he was overwhelmed now. Nervous. All these people looking at him, talking a language he didn't understand. He didn't know what to say. He stared at his hands, folded in his lap.

"Should I give you some choices?" Mulliken asked.

Sam responded with a barely perceptible nod.

"Our goal will be to make you look as symmetrical as possible, to balance out your face," he said. "But we have many things to talk about: your ear, the tongue movement, the eye. The neck's pretty good."

He put his arm around Sam's shoulder. "What do you want?" he asked quietly.

There was so much Sam wanted to say. He didn't know where to start.

"Well, you're really down to the choice of two things," Mulliken said. "We can focus on the face as a whole or the ear, but we can't do both at the same time. If we get the face smaller, the ear will look bigger. Frankly, I just don't know. The face is tough, very tough."

Sam raised his head. He looked at Mulliken with his one good eye.

"I want to fit in," he said in his raspy whisper. "I want to look better."

Mulliken nodded. He pulled the boy closer. "I understand, Sam."

David Lightner had been standing against a wall. Now he moved toward Mulliken, who dropped his arm from Sam's shoulders. "Sam's fourteen years old," David said. "Like you put it, he wants a more symmetrical face. I'm ambivalent. I understand the risk of the whole thing. But this is something Sam wants. We're supporting him."

"Okay, Dad," Mulliken said. Then he turned to the other doctors.

"I think it will be reasonable to focus on the side of his face," Mulliken said. "It will be hard. We'll have to find the facial nerve branches and separate them from the malformation. They look exactly alike."

He shook his head, as if arguing with himself. "The bleeding. Boy! When you're dealing with a pure lymphatic tissue malformation, bleeding is just an annoyance. But if you have these venous components, which he has, it's more than that."

He smiled. "But Sam, I'm going to try."

The goal, Mulliken told the other doctors, was to get the mass down to the bone. If he could eliminate the mass, Sam could have more surgery later to reshape the bone. That surgery would be much easier.

"Another operation?" Debbie asked. "The insurance company's going to really love us."

"Listen," Mulliken said, "you show the insurance company photographs of this boy and there won't be a dry eye in the house."

Debbie and her husband looked at each other.

"Sam?" his father asked.

Sam nodded, more firmly this time. This was his moment. Yes.

Mulliken addressed his patient. "This is going to be tough. We're in for a rough time in the operating room. It's going to be a microscopic dissection, and we're going to need a team." He looked around the room. "Dr. Marler, me, and a few others."

"Your face is going to be swollen for a long time," Mulliken said. "By the time you go back to school, though, you should look considerably better. I'd like to think we can make it fifty percent better.

"Now Sam, is this something you really want?" Sam nodded. Mulliken patted him on the shoulder.

"Let's schedule for July," he told Marler.

"And is this something you want to do, Dr. Mulliken?" David Lightner asked.

Mulliken frowned.

"I'm being blunt," David said, "but we have to know."

"I don't know if 'want' is quite the right word. I *think* we can do it."

He ran his hands over his face. "I *know* we can do it. I wish I could make him perfect. All plastic surgeons search for perfection. But I can't give him that."

"We know he won't be perfect," David said. "That's not our goal."

"Well, your son is in the top echelon in terms of deformity and asymmetry," Mulliken said. "Those are difficult problems to correct. The postoperative course after working with lymphatic malformations of this extent is unpredictable. I can show you pictures of someone who had a similar operation. She has facial nerve paralysis and her face is flat, it doesn't move at all. But she looks better than she did before."

Mulliken hoped to remove a large amount of tissue from the side of Sam's face. He knew the underlying bone would remain misshapen. After the first surgery, there would still be an extraordinary deformity. But removing the tissue was the necessary first step to dealing with the bone.

"I'm bothered that he has to live with this mass," Mulliken told David. "Everyone should have the right to look human."

The Lightners shook hands with Mulliken. The surgeon patted Sam on the back. "I'll see you soon," he said.

Mulliken turned to the other doctors.

"Next case," he said. "Let's go."

Marler lingered a moment.

"Don't worry," she told the Lightners. "You're in good hands."

And then the door closed, and she too was gone.

"Well," said David. "I guess this is the start."

Sam had been disappointed before. He didn't want to get too excited. The Lightners took the elevator to the subbasement, where Sam waited to have the pictures of his head taken. When he walked into the room, a girl with a malformation on her jaw stared at him. She smiled and tugged on her mother's arm. "I bet he sees Dr. Mulliken too," she said loudly.

Debbie nodded. "Yes, he does," she said.

Sam was called for a series of X rays and scans. When he was finished, the technician handed him a basket. "Take one," he said.

Sam looked into the basket and saw cartoon stickers, lollipops, and cupcakes. He glanced at David, who laughed.

"Aw, go on, Sam. Why not? Take one."

If any of the guys in school saw him, he'd feel foolish. He shook his head, stuck his hand in the basket, and pulled out a sticker that he immediately shoved in his pocket. His father pulled him close. Even Debbie was smiling as the Lightners walked to the elevator. On the third floor they waited to see yet another doctor, who would study the films and report back to Mulliken and others on the team.

Once again Sam searched through magazines, and once again he found nothing of interest. He'd give anything for a *Sports Illustrated*. He looked up and saw the girl who'd been in the waiting room with her mother. Sam figured she was eight or nine. He remembered when he was that age. He stood and walked across the room to where the girl was sitting.

"Here," he said. He bent down and handed her the sticker.

"Thanks," she replied.

"Were you here to see Dr. Mulliken?"

The girl nodded shyly.

"Me too." He turned and started to walk away. He stopped. There was something he needed to tell this girl, who more than anyone else in this room knew what he knew.

"Good luck," he told her.

**10** As Debbie Lightner parked the car, she looked at Grant High School and felt as if she were going back in time. When she'd been a student here, she'd had a lot of fun. She hoped the same for Sam, who now followed her across the lawn and up the steps into the main hall.

Sam was coming to Grant in May to register for classes the following September. This was not his neighborhood school; he was applying to be part of the magnet program. Grant was known for its challenging Institute of Science and Math. Both subjects interested him, and came easy to him. As an eighth-grader he had already earned a high school credit for algebra.

The counselor was busy, so the secretary had Sam and Debbie sit in an outer office. There was nothing to read, so Sam looked at the posters from various colleges. He was bored, and waiting here reminded him of waiting in a doctor's office.

"Hi there."

Sam looked up. A man stood in front of him and stuck out his hand. Sam shook it. "Hi," he said.

"Let me welcome you to Grant," the man said. "You're going to love it here. You're going to be a freshman?"

Sam nodded.

The man looked at Debbie. "We have a great bridge program. He's going to love it."

The man turned and walked into an office. "Remember," he called over his shoulder. "It's a great program."

Debbie sensed that the man was talking about a special education class for mentally retarded students. She didn't know how to reply.

When she eventually read about the various programs at Grant, she learned that the bridge program was a "life-skills class" to help students develop reading and writing abilities. The goal was to train them so the community could eventually employ them. Perhaps it was good she hadn't known how to reply to the man.


Later, at home, Debbie got a call from Dr. Marler.

Marler told her that Dr. Mulliken's surgical schedule was usually booked six months in advance, but there was an opening on July 6.

Marler heard nothing from the other end.

"Debbie?"

"I'm here."

"Do you want it?"

Debbie said the family needed to discuss it. She promised to call

Marler the next day. Having an actual date, something to put on the calendar, made it real. And frightening.

That night, the Lightners sat at the dining room table together. Sam was at one end, his father at the other. Debbie sat facing Emily and Nathan.

David played with a pencil, turning it end over end. He wasn't thrilled about his son's undergoing surgery. He remembered what had happened more than a decade before; he didn't want Sam to have to go through a similar experience. But he also recognized that it was not his decision to make alone.

"We have to consider the ramifications of Sam's surgery for the family," David told his children.

"What's a ramification?" Nathan asked.

"I mean that we need to think about how it's going to affect us. We've talked with the doctors, and we know there are dangers. But Dr. Marler told Mommy that if it was her child, she'd want Dr. Mulliken to operate."

"Some things could happen that we wouldn't want to happen," David went on. "We have to be honest about that."

"Like what?" Nathan asked.

"If some of the nerves are damaged, Sam's face could droop," Debbie said. "He'd be paralyzed on one side of his face."

No one looked at Sam.

"And he might bleed a lot during surgery. They think they can control it, but you never know."

David shifted in his chair. "Now that we're three thousand miles away, it's more complicated."

Debbie touched her son's arm. She had asked him the question before; maybe this would be the last time she'd repeat it. "Sam, do you still want to do this?"

Sam, who had been silent all this time, nodded.

"I want to hear it."

"Yes," he said, decisively.

"Okay," David told him. "If I felt something was wrong, I'd intervene. But I have to be honest, it scares me."

"Me too," Nathan said.

"Me too," Emily echoed.

David thought about what the doctors had told him. The mass was like a marble cake, the chocolate swirled in with the vanilla. Nerves, muscle, bone.

He turned to his wife. "We've been through so much, for so long, with Sam," he said. "You want the doctors to say it will all be perfect. But they don't say that. Nothing is simple.

"I worry about the potential damage to Sam. As it stands, he's Sam. He is who he is."

"He'll look different," Emily said. "But Sam is Sam."

"He will always be Sam," said Nathan.

"He is who he is. We don't think there's anything wrong with him." David smiled. "But his situation isn't ideal. He has to cope with a lot because of his face. It's not what Sam wants, but we know it, we feel safe with it. We're talking about doing this to make him look different, and that's scary.

"We're always striving for something better, to improve our lives. Sam is potentially sacrificing a lot. After the surgery, who knows? We just don't know what's going to happen."

"Could something bad happen to him?" Nathan asked.

"Well, like Mommy said, something could go wrong in surgery. And beyond that, we don't know." David leaned forward and stared across the table at Sam. "Any doubts? If you say no, we can call and cancel right now."

"I'm a little nervous," Sam said. "But I like the doctors."

"Well, it scares me," his father said. "It's the unknown."

"Dad, I'm sure," Sam said. "Look what happened at Grant."

"That's what people think about him," Debbie said. "They think he's mentally defective."

Sam mustered his strength. "I want to do this," he repeated.

David placed his hands on the table. He sighed. "We are fearfully and wonderfully made. And very fragile."

Five days before the Lightners were to leave again for Boston, a friend of Debbie's held a backyard party for Sam. Nearly all of the guests had known Sam since he was born. They'd followed his struggles over the years.

At a certain point, the hostess called Sam over to a picnic table. "Sam," she said, "here are a few things for you. I guess you have to be planning a trip all the way to Boston to get things like these."

One by one Sam unwrapped the packages on the table. He was embarrassed, overwhelmed at all the attention—and at the gifts of books, compact discs, and cash.

"We want you to have things you can enjoy on the plane," someone said. "And stuff to keep you busy while you're recovering."

Sam looked out at the faces of the people who loved him. He searched for words to express adequately all that he was feeling: excitement, nervousness, and gratitude. All he needed to say, though, was one word:

"Thanks."

Someone offered a toast. Guests wiped tears from their eyes as they raised their glasses to him.

"Sam," one man said, "you've been waiting for this a long time. You're a brave young man. Good luck. Nothing but good luck."

11    David and Debbie Lightner sat in a small room near the preoperative staging area and listened to the anesthesiologist explain how she would put Sam to sleep and monitor his bodily functions during the operation. When they were alone in the room with Sam, they talked about the weather; about what Emily and Nathan were doing, staying with friends in Portland; about how Sam's beloved Yankees were faring—everything but the reason they were here. Earlier, someone from preop admitting had explained the surgical risks, and the Lightners had signed the necessary papers; now they didn't want to think of these things. David told Sam that when they were back in Portland, they'd go on a long motorcycle ride. And then a nurse in blue surgical scrubs appeared in the doorway.

"It's time to go," she said.

The words startled Sam. This was it, the moment he had been waiting for, and it scared him. He nodded feebly. He thought back to the going-away party in Portland, everyone wishing him luck. "You're going to look so good when you have it done," they had said. "I can't wait to see you when you get back home." "Sam, this is what you've been hoping for."

And now it was time. He lifted himself, his hands trembling slightly on the arms of his chair, and gave his parents a hug. He wanted to look brave in front of the nurse. He moved as casually as he could, with even a bit of a swagger, as if this were no big deal.

"We love you, sweetie." Debbie pulled him close and kissed him softly on his left cheek, on the mass that the doctors planned to target. He could feel the emotion in her hug, and all at once it was a big deal.

He wanted to keep holding her hand, to have her walk with him. Yet he understood he had to take this journey alone. There were things he wanted to say, but he couldn't. He wanted to send her a signal not to worry. He looked at his mother with his right eye, and blinked once. A wink.

"Have a nice sleep." David gave him a hearty pat on the shoulder. He drew Sam close, hugged him tightly, as though refusing to let him walk down the hall and into the unknown. Sam remembered riding on his father's motorcycle, and how he felt so safe when he wrapped his arms around him. He loved this man.

The nurse touched Sam on the shoulder. "We have to go," she said with a smile.

They walked together, silently. The preop holding area had rocking chairs for children to sit in and get comfortable around doctors and nurses until anesthesia took effect. But Sam felt old enough that he didn't need to be babied. He walked into another room, where nurses helped him onto a wheeled operating table. He shook as he lay down, and he admitted that he was scared. A nurse inserted an IV line into his arm, and injected drugs to make him drowsy. Think good thoughts, he told himself. When his eyelids fluttered, he was wheeled into Operating Room 16, which was about the size of a two-car garage, with a fifteen-foot ceiling. It was chilled to sixty-four degrees, to reduce the growth of germs and keep the doctors and nurses comfortable as they worked. Two massive operating lights hung over the table. Light blue sheets covered the patient and the operating table, and the doctors and nurses were the same color.

The door to the scrub room swung open.

"Hello, everyone." Dr. Jennifer Marler entered, her arms dripping with water. The circulating nurse handed her a sterilized towel.

Marler worked the room as if she were at a cocktail party. She talked to each nurse, made sure that everybody was introduced. An operating room, she believed, functioned best when people felt at ease with one another. She always made a point of talking to all the nurses, to make sure they each felt part of the team and understood the surgical plan.

The goal was to cut away the mass on the left side of the boy's face. If all went well, that would set the stage for later work on misshapen bones. But first surgeons had to cut through the overgrown tissue.

A nurse helped Marler into a surgical gown and gloves. The doctor approached the operating table and ran her hands gently across Sam's face, her touch as much a mother's as a doctor's. "We'll take good care of you, Sam," she said.

She put the electrocardiogram leads on his chest, and the blood pressure cuff on his arm. Technically, those were the nurses' responsibilities. But Marler wanted to be there when Sam drifted off to sleep.

"You're falling asleep, now, Sam," a nurse said as she stroked his hair. "Just falling asleep."

The anesthesiologist took her place behind the bank of machines that would control Sam's body during the operation. She turned a knob, and the sound of a pump filled the room. The steady rhythm—one swoosh every two seconds—signified that Sam's lungs were filling with air; the machine was breathing for the unconscious boy.

The circulating nurse, who like all the other nurses had read Sam's medical history, was responsible for everything that came in and out of the room. She stood by the operating table, checking on an IV line that delivered saline solution, to make up blood volume in the face of the bleeding that was sure to follow.

Marler leaned over Sam's body and began suturing his eyelids. She didn't want his eyes to open during surgery, as the swirl of instruments around his face might mean a scratched cornea.

Marler had to stop thinking of Sam Lightner as the boy she had come to know. She had to disassociate herself, and focus on the medical problem before her, on the sheer, impersonal anatomy. If she thought of Sam, an individual and one mother's son, it would be impossible for her to concentrate fully.

As Marler was preparing Sam's face, the scrub room doors swung open again. Dr. John Mulliken entered without a word. Unlike Marler, Mulliken didn't care who the scrub nurse was, as long as the person did the job. He expected all the team to do their job. And do it well. He stopped to study Sam's CAT scans, which hung on a lighted view box.

He held out his hands, and a nurse helped him into gown and gloves. He neared the operating table and looked at his patient. "Good preparation," he told Marler.

For this operation, Mulliken had assembled a team of people who had worked with him for years. They all had thick skins. So it was no surprise to them to see him grasp Sam's head with both hands, and hear him mutter: "It's just so big. It just rolls around."

"I can't have it rolling," he told a nurse. "Stop it."

The nurse searched in a cabinet until she found something that looked like a big doughnut. Sam's head fit in the hole. Mulliken tried moving the head. It didn't budge. "Good," he said.

The swinging doors opened again, and another surgeon, Gary Rogers, joined Mulliken and Marler at the operating table. The blue surgical scrubs covered their bodies, matching caps snug on their heads, masks hiding their mouths and noses. Each wore special glasses outfitted with surgical microscopes that would allow them to examine the tissue of the boy lying before them.

Mulliken walked around the table, studying Sam's head from all angles. Knowing this would be a difficult operation, he had scheduled and performed a warm-up earlier in the morning: repairing a cleft palate in an infant. His hands were limber and steady.

The surgical nurse made final adjustments to the tool-lined trays beside her. The circulating nurse awaited her first order. Mulliken, Rogers, and Marler adjusted their glasses.

Mulliken pointed to a spot near Sam's left ear. That was where he wanted to make the first cut. "Everyone agree?"

Marler and Rogers bent over Sam. "Yes," they said in unison.

Mulliken held out his right hand and asked for a scalpel. He grasped it firmly. "This is going to be a bear."

The scalpel parted the skin, and the flesh gave way to the blade. Then the blood began to flow.

12 The first drop of blood landed on the floor, and Mulliken called for suctioning. Marler used a tool attached to a clear plastic tube. In seconds, the tube resembled a piece of red licorice that snaked across Sam's body, down to the floor, and over to a holding tank where the boy's blood collected.

Rogers held back the skin, allowing Mulliken to proceed. After fifteen minutes, the lead surgeon had opened a three-inch incision. The bleeding hadn't slowed.

He called for a syringe. Marler injected drugs designed to speed clotting into Sam's neck.

The team waited. The blood flowed freely.

The doctors conferred. Mulliken could close now, suture the incision, and end the operation. In the past, whenever Mulliken had encountered such massive bleeding he had closed.

If he continued now, the team would have to work furiously, trying to stay one step ahead of massive bleeding. Even if they exposed the mass, they might never find the nerves that branched out into the tissue.

The mass was a jumble of skin, nerves, lymphatic vessels, veins, and arteries—a big ball of tissue, blood, and other fluid. If Mulliken plunged ahead, it would be like replumbing a house with the water turned on.

Operating Room 16 awaited his decision.

We can't stop here, Marler thought. It would be terrible. We'd be admitting defeat. Push harder, John. Push harder.

Mulliken leaned over Sam's body. "Let's go on," he finally said.

The circulating nurse went to a phone and punched in the four-digit number for the hospital's blood bank. There were six units of blood in a cooler in the operating room. The plastic bag holding a unit of blood that dripped from an IV line into Sam's right arm was already half empty. The nurse told the bank to set aside an additional six. Sam might bleed so much that the doctors would have to replace his entire blood supply.

As the three doctors worked, the suctioning line continued to carry away the boy's blood. Each time the scalpel moved, it sliced a blood vessel. The team went through countless surgical towels and sponges, soaking up blood so they could see where they were.

Mulliken called for the Bovie, a device resembling a dental drill that electrically cauterizes blood vessels. In a normal body, the machine helps stop bleeding, and surgery can be almost bloodless. Marler held the Bovie in her right hand.

There was the sound of sizzling. A plume of smoke rose over Sam's head. But the bleeding continued.

A nurse walked behind the team and hung another bag of blood on the IV line. "Jesus Christ," Mulliken muttered.

The team pulled back skin. They could see the edge of the mass. "Easy," Mulliken said. "Easy."

The side of the boy's face oozed blood. Drops continued to splatter on the floor. A red stain spread through the surgical sheets. Nurses called for more towels. Within minutes, one after another was soaked through.

The insides of Marler's shoes were wet with Sam's blood. She asked for a new pair of socks.

At this point, if they were to go ahead, Mulliken saw only one option: stitching each blood vessel closed. He called for needles.

While Marler continued cutting, Rogers used the Bovie, and Mulliken started stitching. The surgical nurse supplied him packet after packet of stitches.

When Mulliken's fingers tired, Marler took over, then Rogers. The bleeding slowed to a trickle. The team had tied more than two hundred stitches. They pulled Sam's skin back slowly and covered it with a towel to keep it moist. The mass was exposed.

Mulliken looked to an information board in a corner of the operating room. Sam had gone through three units of blood, and the team hadn't even reached the heart of the operation. He stepped away from the table and told Marler and Rogers to clean up the area surrounding the mass. He needed a break.

Surgical coverings hid Sam's body and most of his face, leaving only the mass of tissue exposed under the glare of surgical lights. With the skin pulled back, it looked like raw meat.

Even exposed, the mass was still a mystery. X rays don't show soft tissue. So there was no way of knowing how invasive the mass was, or what it was wrapped around. A single nerve from the brain divides into five branches that spread out to control the side of the face. The mass could be resting atop those nerve branches, or it could be spread under them. Or the nerves could pass right through it. If Mulliken guessed wrong and cut a nerve, Sam would lose the ability to close his right eye, wrinkle his forehead, smile.

When Mulliken returned to the operating room, the blood had slowed to a trickle. The team would hunt for nerve branches with an electric probe. If they touched a nerve, Sam's face would twitch.

The circulating nurse pulled a thick anatomy book from a shelf. She turned to a page that detailed the facial nerves and left it open on a table so the team could refer to it. But it would do them no good. In this part of Sam's body, nothing was as it should be.

The team began removing bits of the mass. The bleeding resumed.

After an hour, Mulliken took another break. He headed to the scrub room, removed his gown and gloves, and sat down in a chair. The pressure was intense, physically and mentally, and the team had to work in shifts: when one surgeon tired, another would take the scalpel. Mulliken leaned his head back and closed his eyes. After fifteen minutes, he stirred and returned, in fresh scrubs and gloves, to the operating table.

"How's it going?" he asked Marler and Rogers.

"The scars from his previous surgery aren't making things easy," she said.

"Don't relax," Mulliken said. The biggest danger, as they all knew, was in getting too comfortable, careless, and mistaking as tissue something that was in fact the edge of a hidden nerve. "Have you found it yet?"

"We think we found the region."

"I *know* the region," he said. "I want the nerve."

Mulliken liked to talk out loud in the operating room. Surgery was about making choices: Do I go this way, or that? Talking about those choices aloud helped clarify how to proceed.

Now Mulliken took over, and Marler took a break. She wanted to shower and get something to eat, and she planned to call her husband to tell him she wouldn't be home until late.

When she returned about twenty minutes later, she found Mulliken and Rogers frustrated. They hadn't found any branches of the main nerve, and the operation was entering its fifth hour.

The kid was still bleeding, and near the end of his fourth unit of blood.

As Mulliken mopped up more blood, he was doubting his ability to help Sam. Perhaps it had been a mistake to take the case. He told the team there were two choices: Cut even faster, to speed up the operation, but thereby increase the risk of destroying part of the nerve. Or close.

"I've been here before," he admitted. "I think we should close up."

Marler disagreed. "Let's keep going."

"Then you take over," Mulliken said. "You wanted to bring him here, you look for the nerve."

Marler took the probe. The anatomy here was like nothing she'd seen, in real life or in any textbook. She wished the students in the anatomy class she taught at Harvard Medical School could be looking over her shoulder now. Even for her this was a learning experience. And while she was energized by the challenge, there was also the life at stake: Sam continued to bleed; more than two hundred sponges and towels had soaked up his blood so far. The tank where the suction line emptied sloshed red.

"I've got something," Marler said at one point. "This is scar tissue like you have never seen." Slowly, carefully, she applied the electric probe again, and a muscle twitched.

"You got it?" Mulliken asked.

"I think so. But I can't distinguish nerve from scar tissue. It's all entangled. And it's deeper than it should be. I'm afraid to dissect any further."

Mulliken traded places with her. He peered into the side of Sam's face and held out his right hand. A nurse gave him a scalpel. He touched the mass with the tip of the scalpel.

"I can't budge the nerve from the scar tissue, either," he said. "It really is entangled in it."

Marler used the probe. Sam's forehead moved. "Every time I dissect, I'm worried," she said.

"It's bad, but we've come this far," Mulliken said. "We've got to get it out."

Rogers assisted with suctioning and controlling the bleeding so Mulliken could see where the nerve might lie.

"Let's stimulate around what we think is the edge," Mulliken said. Test. nothing. Test. Nothing. Test. Finally, a reaction.

Mulliken cut. "It should be under here."

He sighed. They were more than six hours into the operation.

The three doctors focused on a tiny spot within a mass the size of a quarter.

"I think there's a branch up here." Mulliken asked for the probe, and tried to work his way up the tiny nerve he'd located, searching for the main branch.

He applied the probe again.

"Come on, people," he snapped. "Talk to me."

"His forehead moved," said Marler.

Mulliken tried again. "Bingo," he said.

The team moved out from that nerve, searching for other branches.

"We have to see it, get around it," Mulliken said. "It goes right through this mass."

"What are we going to do when we're there?" Marler asked. "Could we get the malformation off and then go back and do a nerve graft?"

"No. We can't even find all the nerves. All this time, and we can't even get to the nerves."

A sudden spurt of blood hit Marler's blue gown. The scalpel had nicked a branch of the carotid artery.

"Bleeder!" Mulliken yelled for clamps and sutures to stanch the flow. The surgical nurse didn't move fast enough for him. "Come on," he shouted, working frantically. "We got a real bleeder here! Oh, Jesus."

The fifth and sixth bags of blood drained as though they had holes. The blood loss could send Sam into cardiac arrest. He was close to death. Mulliken shifted the boy's head, stitched, and then grabbed another instrument and stitched again. The bleeding slowed.

The hallway outside Operating Room 16 emptied. It was ten-thirty p.m., and janitors cleaned the surrounding rooms, readying them for the next day. In the entire hospital, only one surgery continued, the one in Operating Room 16.

The team reoriented itself. They suctioned off blood and again looked for nerves.

Mulliken probed. "Let's get going here," he said. "We're losing time."

He asked the surgical nurse for a tool covered with green dye and mapped the nerve branches on the exposed tissue. Anything between the green lines could be cut. At the lines, as close to the nerve as possible, they tested again. They thought they'd found most of the nerves, but they wouldn't be sure until Sam regained consciousness and tried to move.

They began cutting. Small pieces, the size of toenail clippings. Then more pieces, some of them the size of marbles.

Marler dissected the area under Sam's chin. "That should go," she said as she pulled out a large chunk.

Mulliken pulled the flap of skin back over Sam's face. "He looks a lot better," he said.

He folded the flap back down. "Folks," he said, "we're down to the bone."


Sam's blood had lost the ability to clot. A nurse replenished the IV line with a seventh bag.

"He's bleeding from every little hole—we've got to get out of here," Mulliken said. "Close."

Rogers and Marler started stitching the flap of skin back to the side of Sam's face.

"His chin is going to look awesome," Marler said.

"Not a bad way to start high school," Mulliken observed.

He stepped away from the operating table, removing his gloves, mask, and gown. At a table in a nearby room he sat and filled out forms. He noted the time: midnight. The surgery had lasted nearly thirteen hours. Once he'd finished the paperwork, he walked out of the surgical area and down silent, empty hallways. In the surgery waiting room, he found Sam's parents, both of them dozing. When he cleared his throat, they stirred.

"All is well," he told the Lightners. "Everything's fine."

"How'd it go?" David asked.

Mulliken sat down and ran a hand across his face. "It was very difficult," Mulliken said. "Maybe the most difficult surgery I've ever performed. At times we were very discouraged. But no one wanted to give up."

He yawned.

"The next step will be fixing the mandible bone, probably next summer. That won't be a problem."

Debbie and David Lightner looked at each other. They clasped hands.

"You know, Doctor, when I talk with you, I realize how used to Sam's face we were," David said. "To me, to us, he's always been just Sam, just a kid with a big old head."

Mulliken nodded.

"What's sad," David continued, "is that the rest of the world can't see beyond the face."

There was an awkward silence. The Lightners weren't sure what to do or say.

Debbie Lightner finally spoke. "Thank you."

Mulliken smiled. "You're welcome," he said. He turned and disappeared.

**13** The doors to Operating Room 16 opened, and two Intensive Care nurses, dispatched from another area of the hospital, wheeled Sam Lightner's gurney slowly from the center of the room.

They maneuvered the gurney around a nurse who was tossing bloody sponges and towels into a bucket. Another nurse fished out the towels, hung them on the side of the bucket and counted out loud, making sure that all were accounted for. A third nurse counted and catalogued the surgical tools, checking them off a master list. In the corner, a nurse pulled a stool to a narrow desk and put the final touches on official reports, glancing at the wall clock to record that the boy was leaving the room just after twelve-thirty a.m. on July 7, 2000.

A thick bandage—brilliant white except for the streak of red left by blood still oozing through sutures on his neck—swathed Sam's head. He looked as if he'd been in a serious accident. His closed eyes were puffy, as if he'd been struck in the face. An IV line pumped painkillers and other drugs into his body. An anesthesiologist walked beside the gurney, checking to make sure that Sam's blood pressure didn't drop, that he didn't go into cardiac arrest during the move.

In the operating room Dr. Marler took off her surgical gown and gloves and deposited them in a plastic bag filled with surgical debris. Her legs trembled, as they did after every long procedure. Only when such operations were over did she realize she'd been standing for so long.

She walked around the operating room and thanked each nurse for the great work they'd done. She shook hands and patted them on the back, and said she hoped to work with them again.

She then hurried after Sam's gurney, reaching the elevator just in time. She wanted to accompany Sam to Intensive Care, and meet with the Lightners and reassure them that all was well. After that rough surgery, Sam's head was swollen to the size of a basketball. Although his parents had been prepared by a nurse liaison who had been checking in on them during the course of the operation, Marler knew they would be shocked when they saw him.

Part of this, she admitted to herself, was ego. She wanted to tell somebody how well the surgery had gone. And she wanted the Intensive Care nurses to feel that same excitement. As caring and conscientious as she knew they were, she wanted the nurses to think of him not as the kid in bed F-14, but as Sam Lightner. They were playing an important role in his recovery, and in a case that Marler considered very significant. She didn't want anyone who wasn't aware of the case to be taking care of Sam.

In the ICU, Marler told the nurses to make sure his head was always supported. If it somehow dropped off the bed, the weight could cause a spinal injury.

The swelling would reduce in a month's time. This first stage might make Sam look fifty percent better, but fifty percent improvement on a facial deformity such as his still left a lot of work undone.

Marler left the ICU and went to put on new scrubs, as she always did before meeting parents of children who'd been operated on. She didn't want them to see blood on her clothes and be reminded that it came from their child. Then she went to see the Lightners.

Marler asked if they had any questions. Unlike some parents Marler had met, Debbie and David Lightner never seemed rattled or nervous. Even in the anxious moments before surgery, when they signed consent forms, they seemed calm. Perhaps they had come to terms with the life that Sam had been forced to lead thus far.

Marler explained that Sam was heavily sedated and not expected to stir for at least the next thirty-six hours. She suggested the Lightners return to their hotel and sleep late this day. They didn't need to worry. She gave them each a hug.

During the day, a Friday, the Lightners checked on Sam, who remained asleep. When they returned Saturday, a nurse said he was responding to commands. They went to his room and called his name. He motioned for the paper and pencil on the bed table, and slowly wrote out a question: *What day is it?*

July 8, his mother said.

He wrote another question: *What happened to the 6th and 7th?*

A nurse told him he'd been in surgery, and then recovering. Sam's eyes closed and he appeared to fall back asleep.

"Sam," his mother called. He didn't respond.

A nurse wheeled a machine over to Sam's bed, from which a small computer was suspended in front of him. Before his surgery, a speech and language specialist had programmed the machine so that Sam could communicate. There were five responses: *I hurt; I need to go to the bathroom; Yes; No;* and—at David's request—*Bring me a woman.* Sam had only to lift a finger and push a button to answer.

"Sam," Debbie called again. He opened his eyes only briefly.

She leaned over him. "Sam," she said. "How do you feel?"

He slowly raised a finger and punched the button for *I hurt.* The pain, the nurses had told Debbie, would be severe for at least three weeks. But he was on the mend, doing great after such an ordeal.

Dr. Marler now joined the Lightners. She gave both parents a hug. The three of them looked at Sam. A ventilator still breathed for him, its line hooked into the hole in his throat.

Marler wanted to check on Sam's nerves without alarming his parents. She felt confident about the branches leading to eye and forehead. But what about the branch to the mouth? She had to know if all this was intact. Sam seemed to be sound asleep, and she didn't want to wake him.

"Has he been awake?" she asked.

"Yes," Debbie said. "When I said something to him he moved."

"Can you make him smile? I'd like to see if he can smile."

Debbie moved her head close to her son's. "Sam," she called. "Sam."

The ventilator whooshed steadily.

Marler saw the boy's eyelids flutter. Good sign.

"Try again," she told Debbie.

"Sam," his mother said. "I need you to smile for me."

There was no response.

"Sam. Smile."

Then, gradually, one edge of his mouth seemed to curl. And Sam Lightner smiled.

Mulliken stopped by several times the next few days to examine Sam. The boy's face was healing quite well, he said.

Even with painkillers, Sam's face hurt. When he shifted on the pillow, the slightest pressure made him wince. He tried to make out his face reflected on the televison glass. But the angle was wrong. He couldn't see a thing. He relied on his parents and the nurses, who kept telling him he was doing so well.

Eight days after the operation, an internist came to remove the bandages around the boy's head. Debbie Lightner (now there alone, as David had returned to Portland to work) was warned to be realistic; the unveiling would be anticlimatic, even disappointing. Sam's face had taken a beating in surgery, and the buildup of internal fluids would make his face look distorted, perhaps more than it did before. For the next two months, he would have to wear an elastic mask at night to force his face into shape and to combat the swelling. The results, the doctor said, would be seen only in late September or early October.

Even so, Sam could hardly wait to view his new face. His mother stood by the side of his bed, and helped him sit up and lean back on a pillow.

As the doctor unwrapped the bandages, Sam could feel cool air on his face. He looked at his mother, trying to gauge what she thought. She smiled. The doctor moved away from the bed, and Debbie moved in to help Sam stand. He was unsteady, like a colt learning to walk. She guided him to the bathroom and stopped in front of the mirror.

He gathered the strength to look at himself. A mirror had always meant seeing his flaws. Dr. Mulliken's message played in his head: *Don't get your hopes up.* That had been Sam's mantra for much of his life, especially when surgeon after surgeon had turned him away. He had learned to never get his hopes up.

He raised his eyes and looked at the reflection. He didn't see his mother standing behind him. He didn't see the internist to one side, or the nurse who had quietly slipped into the room. He listened to the voice in his head: *Smaller. Point under the chin gone. Rounder. Smoother.*

He turned his face to the right, to examine the left side in the mirror. For the first time in more than a year, he could see his left ear, huge and distorted: the tissue mass that had obscured it was gone.

*The surgery had worked.*

He turned from the mirror to his mother. He smiled, raised his hand, and gave her a thumbs-up sign.

In mid-July, doctors released Sam from the hospital. They asked that he stay in Boston for a few days in case infection set in. He wasn't scheduled to see Mulliken again until the following summer, when he would return for another surgery, to reshape the bone in his face.

Painkillers made the days bearable; Sam and Debbie explored a museum, took in a movie, and went out for pizza. They went to Fenway Park, but the only tickets available for that day's game didn't seem to be in a very comfortable section. Sam told his mother he was too tired after all the sightseeing. They returned to the hotel, where Debbie read magazines and Sam watched television.

The day before they were supposed to fly back to Portland, Sam woke up tired and weak. He was lying in bed, touching his new face, when he felt a lump on his chin. He thought the worst—that this was a new growth, that he'd end up back in the hospital because the mass had again roared to life, as it had the year before.

He told his mother, and she too felt something on his chin, but she told Sam not to worry. Then she called the hospital. A nurse told her to bring Sam in.

Debbie and Sam sat anxiously in the waiting area. The trip, the surgery, the anticipation of going home, and now this pain and fear: it was all too much for Sam. He leaned against his mother and cried tears of frustration and pain, of hopelessness. He didn't care who saw him.

By chance, Dr. Marler was passing through the area on her way to the laboratory. She saw the Lightners and came over.

"What are you doing here?" she asked. "I thought you'd be back in Portland."

Debbie explained the problem, Sam's pain, the lump on his chin.

Marler knelt beside him. "How do you feel?"

He couldn't speak. He shrugged. He cried.

Marler wiped away the tears with her fingers. "It'll be okay, Sam. Here, let me look at your chin."

He raised his chin and stared in her eyes. She sat on the bench next to him and ran her fingers along his chin, feeling for the incisions she had made.

"This isn't a mass," she said. "Don't worry. It's just a problem with fluid draining."

Marler checked with a receptionist and found an empty examination room. Once in the room with the Lightners, she turned the lights low to calm Sam. She administered a local anesthetic, and waited for it to take effect.

She touched his chin. He did not flinch. She reached for a syringe to drain the fluid from his chin. She wanted him to be distracted when the needle pierced his skin.

"Sam," she said, "could you send me a photograph of yourself when you get home? I'd like to have something to remember you by." His photo, she hoped, would join the gallery on her office wall—the pictures of children who had touched her during her medical career, who had come to her for help.

She finished her work, and told Debbie to give Sam pain medication.

He'd be fine now, ready to travel the next morning.

Marler spread her arms wide and pulled Sam close. As she hugged him, tears rolled down her cheeks.

**14** The trip home, on July 20, was exhausting, and Sam did not feel well. He slept fitfully as the plane crossed the country. At one point, Debbie thought he was running a fever. When they landed in Portland, Sam slowly made his way up the aisle and into the terminal. When he saw a cluster of balloons, he smiled. And there were Emily and Nathan, and the family friend who had taken care of them until David returned. They approached cautiously, not sure how tightly they could hug him.

"You look really different," Emily told him. "Your face is round and curvy."

It was time to celebrate. Sam showed his new face to friends and relatives. Everyone agreed that the surgery had been a success, well worth the risk. She felt that he looked good.

But he didn't feel all that well. He was tired, listless, and stayed in bed until late. He didn't want to be with his friends, didn't even want to watch television with his brother and sister. His skin was pale. Debbie knew something was wrong. She called Dr. Campbell, who had been designated as the follow-up surgeon.

Sam sat silently in the car as his parents drove to Emanuel Hospital. He moved like an old man getting out of the car, and barely picked up his feet on the way to the medical offices. Once in the waiting room, he fell into the first chair he found. He didn't care about the magazines on the table nearby. He closed his eyes and curled his legs under himself. Sweat glistened on his forehead.

When the receptionist called his name he pushed himself with effort out of the chair and followed her to an examination room. His parents had to walk especially slowly behind. Sam climbed onto the examination table and let his head sag forward. Debbie stood close by, and ran her hands through his brown hair. After a knock, the door opened and Campbell came in, carrying a file. He scanned a few sheets and turned to Sam.

"Sambo, you old dog," he said. "How are you?"

"He's not feeling well," Debbie Lightner said. "He had a temperature of about a hundred this morning. And he seems so tired. I don't know if it's from the trip home or what. But he just doesn't seem himself."

"I know the feeling," Campbell said. Six weeks earlier, he told the Lightners, he had had surgery for a clogged artery. "And I can tell you, no surgeon wants to have surgery."

Campbell put the file down, washed his hands in the sink, and returned to the examination table. He leaned close to Sam.

"They did a great job back there," he said. "That mass is much smaller." He stepped back. "Sam, you look better than good, you look great."

"Sambo," he said gently, "let me take a good look at you."

Sam raised his face.

"He's a little swollen," Campbell told Sam's parents, "but that's to be expected. Sam, how about lying down for me?"

He ran his hands over the boy's face, checked the file, then walked over and felt Sam's forehead for the tube the Boston surgeons had sutured under his scalp.

"I think it's time we take that drain tube out. Now, this might hurt, Sam. But it's going to be over quickly."

Sam tried to sit up, struggling, kicking his legs. "No," he moaned. "No."

His father held Sam's legs. His mother grasped his arms. "Hold still, honey," she said. Sam squirmed to resist. Campbell yanked twice and drew out a clear line from the side of his face.

"Okay, big boy," he said. "It's over."

Sam sat up, tears streaking his face. He struggled to catch his breath. Campbell had him lie down again. He kept a hand on his shoulder, patting him to calm him.

"He's lost ten pounds," Debbie said. "Some, I know, is from the surgery. But—"

Campbell interrupted. "So he's not eating well?"

"No."

Campbell shook his head. "I think I may have to put him in the hospital."

"No," croaked Sam. "No. Please."

Campbell placed a hand on Sam's shoulder while he talked to Sam's parents. "I want him there for a day or two. We'll do a blood culture and get a blood count, and give him some IV antibiotics. I'm sure that blood count will be way off. I think he has an infection. We can't take any risks."

Sam sobbed. After all the painful days he'd spent bedridden in Boston, he was headed back to the hospital.

"I know you're not happy about it," Campbell said. "I know you want to be at home. But you can get real sick, real fast. Those germs could spread through your body if we don't catch them now." He didn't want to frighten the boy further, but the truth was that an untreated septic infection could be life-threatening.

Campbell patted Sam's shoulder. "I'm sorry, Sam. I really am. But don't give up—we'll lick this."

Sam could only cry.

"At least we're here, not in Boston," David told his son.

"And it will only be a couple days," Debbie added.

Campbell moved aside to let the Lightners comfort their son.

"I'm going to call someone from the floor to come get him," he said quietly. "I want him to be looked at right away. I'll write up some papers and see him before the end of the day. Don't worry. This is just a precaution."

After two days in the hospital, Sam's temperature dropped, and as Campbell had promised, he checked out of Emanuel and went home. Hospital regulations required that Sam be taken by wheelchair to the front driveway. Once he had raised himself out of the wheelchair and settled into the family's car, Sam told himself that he never wanted to come back here.

At home Sam closed himself in the bathroom and looked in the mirror. The swelling had receded, and the left side of his face was noticeably reduced. The bottom of his chin, once distended and pointed, was flat and smooth. Even his left eye seemed to be in a more normal position. His parents had told him he looked great.

But when he scrutinized his face the way he knew strangers would, he realized that he didn't look dramatically different from how he looked before the surgery. The skin on the left side of his face, while relieved of some of the huge mass of tissue that had supported it, still rose domelike over the deformed bone beneath. His jaw remained out of alignment, and it still distorted his mouth and teeth. Removing the mass had further exposed his left ear, which was large, spongy, and misshapen. The surgeons would turn to all those problems the next year. But in a matter of weeks, he would be entering Grant High School.

**15** The day arrived. The boy sat on the living room sofa, lost in his thoughts. His parents were at work. He watched his brother and sister lounging around, enjoying the last two weeks of summer vacation. Sam couldn't sit still. He looked at the clock, waiting for his mother to come home and take him to Grant. Today he would officially join the class of 2004. When his sister asked him a question, he ignored her. He had too many things on his mind.

He went to his bedroom and paused at the door. Should he take down the toy license plate with his name on it, he asked himself. After all, he wasn't a kid anymore. From his closet he pulled out a brand-new shirt. He'd already showered, and now he put the clean shirt on. He walked downstairs and studied himself in the mirror. His hair was neatly combed, except for one last stubborn strand. He smoothed it down into place.

In the kitchen he looked at the list of chores posted on the refrigerator door. For his five-dollar-a-week allowance, Sam was expected to throw the dirty clothes down the chute to the basement, clean the bathroom countertop, and sweep the bathroom floor. He'd done all this week's chores, and cleaned up the basement and vacuumed the upstairs hallway.

Just as he heard his mother's car pull into the driveway, the telephone rang. One of his middle school classmates was calling to let Sam know that he and two other boys who had gathered at his house were ready for their ride.

Sam was ready too. But when he touched his neck and pulled his hand away, there was blood on his finger.

Not today. Not on this day. Please.

"Mom."

He pointed to his neck. Blood oozed from one of his stitches. He dabbed at it with a paper towel.

"Mom!"

His mother searched for a Band-Aid.

"No one will see this," she said as she pressed the strip over the stitch. "Don't worry."

They got into the car and Debbie drove off, turning through tree-lined streets. At one house she pulled over to the curb, and three strapping young men came off the porch. They squeezed into the backseat, while Sam sat next to his mother in front. He looked like a little brother along for the ride.

Traffic clogged the streets around Grant, so Debbie Lightner parked a few blocks away. Sam and his friends stepped out of the car and headed toward the school.

Sam touched the Band-Aid on his neck. He adjusted his shirt collar, trying to hide it. His friends, who towered over him, kept up a constant conversation. At the school entrance they all grew quiet.

Sam pulled one of the doors open and stepped into the front hall. Linoleum floors. Trophy cases. Metal lockers. Noise and laughter and chaos and all the urgency of being a teenager.

An adult shouted instructions, and some students formed a rough line. Sam's friends disappeared into the crowd, and then reappeared, talking with friends in the line. They didn't pay any attention to Sam.

The line grew longer and more orderly, and was directed toward the cafeteria, where students would receive their identification cards and schedules. Teachers and other adults herded the students along, repeating instructions. One teacher brought out a fan to keep everyone cool.

Sam watched students arrive and walk past him to the end of the line. He turned to his left, so that no one could see the left side of his face. Even the students standing next to him seemed unaware of his presence.

"Hey there."

Sam turned. A man motioned to him and then walked over.

"How're you doing?" the man asked as he stuck out his hand.

"Fine." Sam shook hands, but he wondered who the man was.

The man raised his hand and seemed to gesture toward Sam's face, then think better of it. His hand dropped to his side. "You don't have to wait here in line," he said. "I mean . . . Let me take you down the back way." He rattled a set of keys. "I can get you in and out of here in a couple minutes. Otherwise you're going to be here for a couple hours. You shouldn't have to wait out here in front of everyone. I know how you must be feeling right now."

The man put his arm around Sam's shoulder. "Let's go. You don't need this."

Sam's response was colored, as such things are, by everything that had come before. The years of living with his deformity. The decision to risk a life-threatening surgery. The choices to take a big chance and confront life head-on.

"I am Sam," the nurse had posted over his isolette when he was born. "Sam I am."

Sam wriggled out from under the man's arm. "No," he said.

"What?"

"I'll wait with the rest of the students," Sam said.

"But you don't have to."

"I'll wait," Sam said firmly. "This is where I belong."

The line moved, and Sam watched the man walk away. He couldn't change his mind now. Sam moved, like everyone else, step by shuffling step, toward the cafeteria. The line proceeded to a registration station along the cafeteria wall.

Brian, a friend of Sam's from Gregory Heights, saw him in line and hurried over. He handed him a piece of paper with a locker number and combination written on it. Students shared lockers at Grant, and Brian, who had arrived earlier, had claimed a locker and requested Sam as a partner.

Someone touched Sam's shoulder, and he turned to see a friend from his neighborhood.

"I was thinking about you all summer," she said. "I wondered if you had the surgery."

She looked at him. "Oh," she said. "You look great."

As Sam examined his schedule, he heard somebody call out his name.

A girl he knew from eighth grade bustled up and leaned close. "Can I see your schedule?" she asked.

He handed her the sheet of paper.

"Sam," she squealed. "We got word-processing together."

He blushed.

The line moved forward. At the station for yearbook pictures, Sam puzzled over what picture package to order. He selected the one that offered two extra prints. One would go to Dr. Mulliken, the other to Dr. Marler.

He handed the order form to the photographer, who told him where to sit and how to pose. "Okay, kiddo," the photographer said. "Here we go."

Sam looked straight ahead. This was for the yearbook. This was for history. He smiled. Broadly. And a brilliant flash illuminated his face.

In September, on the first day of class, Sam went to the school basement and waited in front of a locked door. He checked his schedule. This was the right place. He stood on his tiptoes and looked in the window. The room was empty. How could he mess up on the first day? Other freshmen arrived, but none would talk, all of them embarrassed that they had made a stupid mistake. A bell rang, and a teacher hurried down the steps.

"The schedule is wrong," he told the students. "Follow me."

He led the group upstairs. Being with a group made Sam feel less foolish.

"This is dumb," a boy near Sam grumbled.

"No kidding."

"What's your name?" the boy asked.

"Sam. What's yours?"

"Good to meet you."

"Hi."

After his first week at school, Sam looked at his face in the mirror, and decided that he looked better than ever. He realized he had been wrong about one thing. His goal had once been to be nothing more than an anonymous freshman, to blend in and be ignored. He didn't want that anymore.

He couldn't wait to get to school that next Monday. The classwork seemed challenging, but it wasn't too hard. The teachers were cool. The man who taught history had a last name that was difficult to pronounce; he told the kids to call him "Mr. G."

When Sam walked to his locker he saw a sign announcing the football team's first game of the season. Sam *was* going to that. At lunch he listened to some people talking about a school dance. He wasn't so sure about that.

On September 17, Sam stayed home from school. He felt sick, and didn't even get out of bed. His mother thought it might be a touch of the flu. He returned to Grant within a few days, seemingly on the mend. But Debbie noticed that he wobbled when he walked, almost as if he had been drinking.

"How are you feeling?" she asked him one night.

"Okay," he told her.

"You looked like you were having trouble walking."

"I've been feeling kind of dizzy."

Debbie pointed to his left arm. "Why are you doing that?"

His arm looked stiff, and he held it from the side of his body at an unnatural angle.

"I don't know," Sam said. "I didn't know I was even doing it."

The next day Debbie saw that he was again wobbling and doing that strange thing with his left arm. She made an appointment for him with Dr. Campbell.

The doctor weighed Sam, looked at his records, and said that

Sam was too thin. But other than that he found nothing wrong with the boy. Perhaps he had some kind of virus. He prescribed antibiotics.

At school the next day Sam asked a teacher if he could leave a class early. He gathered his books and went into the hall, hoping he wouldn't throw up. He used the phone in the main office to call his mother at work. She drove to the school, took Sam home, and put him to bed.

"I really feel dizzy, Mom," he said. Then he threw up.

Debbie took him to an ear, nose, and throat specialist. He too found nothing wrong. Maybe Sam had problems within his distorted left ear. The ear might be draining, and that could be upsetting Sam's equilibrium. The doctor prescribed eardrops.

They had no effect. And the dizzy spells continued. Sam couldn't keep food down.

He started missing school.

One day.

Then two.

When his parents visited Grant for a parent-teacher meeting, his teachers said Sam was a great student. He was making friends. Everyone wanted him back.

Three.

Four.

Sam wanted to be at school. But when he stood up he felt dizzy. And during the last two days a weak headache had grown stronger.

As September drew to a close, Sam Lightner had missed a week of school, and he felt drained. His left arm seemed to have a life of its own, hanging at that weird angle. He would pull it back and thirty minutes later see it acting up again.

Emily and Nathan went to school. His parents went to work.

He told them he could stay home alone. One morning he felt a pain in his head. Debbie called from work to check on him, and told him to take over-the-counter painkillers. They didn't relieve the pain. And each hour he felt worse.

This was a different kind of headache. When he leaned his head back, it felt as if something was pushing deep within it.

Deep within his brain.

# the brain

*When it comes to the brain,*
*don't listen to anyone but me.*

DR. MONICA WEHBY TO
DAVID AND DEBBIE LIGHTNER

**16** Dr. Monica Wehby walks quietly down the dark stairway in her suburban Portland home. She doesn't turn the light on because she doesn't want to rouse her husband and four young children, all asleep upstairs. Besides, she gets up often enough in the middle of the night that she knows her way around in the dark. If she's not kept awake fretting about her young patients and the decisions she has to make for them, her own children call for her. Or the phone next to her side of the bed rings, and a voice on the other end has a question, or informs her that there's an emergency and she's needed at the hospital. If a child in Oregon, southwestern Washington, or much of Idaho has a problem with his head or brain, he's likely to end up at Emanuel Hospital and under her care.

Early morning in her home is the most precious part of her day. She owns these moments when no one intrudes. The instant she walks out the door, everything changes. Wehby, a pediatric neuro-surgeon, works in what is considered the most demanding, intense, and emotionally draining of surgical specialties. When she advises eager medical students, she tells them the truth: If they don't have an all-consuming passion for the field, if they'd be just as happy doing something else, they're better off finding another track. The long hours, the weekend work, the constant pressures of dealing with young lives hanging in the balance exacts a toll as no other specialty does.

Wehby has no margin for error in her work. If she cuts too much, the kid bleeds out. If she cuts too little, the tumor wins. Whatever she does, she will affect a child—for good or ill—for the rest of his life. Her patients aren't seventy-five-year-olds with rich histories, but kids who are learning to walk, who have yet to drive a car. And while mortality is a reality for everyone, the death of a child is always bitter, a reminder that doctors are not miracle workers. The heart of even the toughest surgeon is bruised when a child breathes his last. Wehby lives with that pressure, thrives on it, a surgeon willing to venture into small and unforgiving areas of human anatomy where there is no such thing as a second chance. If she misjudges and shaves off as little as a microscopic bit of the brain stem, the child's eyes no longer work. If she tears a blood vessel, the child has a stroke. If one of her brain shunts—installing one is by now a routine procedure—malfunctions, the child will die within hours or suffer severe damage.

As soon as Wehby reaches the hospital, everyone will want something from her. Her office is wherever she happens to be—the elevator; a hallway; occasionally, the bathroom. "Dr. Wehby, just a moment for a consult." "Dr. Wehby, could you just look at this scan." "Dr. Wehby, they want you in the ICU." "Dr. Wehby, we're scared." People count on her quick mind, pure heart, and strong and sure hands, which never shake, not even in the most harrowing of operations.

She enters the front hall. In the living room to her left is a piano that she never has time to play. The only night she has free to watch television is Sunday. She reads only the weekend newspapers, and likes to check the horoscope to see what the day holds for a Taurus. She hasn't been on a real vacation in five years. When she leaves town, patients and office staff track her down.

She pads into the kitchen for her first cup of coffee of the day. She never eats breakfast. Lunch, at best, is a hit-and-miss affair, something grabbed on the run. She makes it through her fifteen-hour days fueled by coffee and inexpensive chocolate candy she nibbles when she stops in her private office.

She considers this morning's case—a nine-month-old girl whose face she will reshape during a five-hour operation. She's one of only two surgeons in Oregon qualified to undertake such a reconstruction. It's not a particularly hard procedure, although she worries about a large vein that runs down the center of the baby's brain. If she damages the vein, the child could bleed to death in thirty seconds.

Wehby has only three fears: heights, being trapped in an enclosed place, and bleeding—especially bleeding in babies. A year ago, when she operated on the brain of another nine-month-old, the blood flowed as if a drain had been unplugged.

Every standard procedure failed. Wehby was sure the baby was going to die. Her hands almost started shaking. She stepped back from the table, collected herself, and resorted to a series of surgical techniques that did not require applying pressure to stop the blood. Everything turned out fine. But the sight of that blood lingered, and the case still haunts her, reminding her that all hell can break out in an instant in the operating room.

Wehby wears light-green surgical scrubs, a black pager on her waist and a strand of pearls—her trademark since medical school—around her neck. She's a petite woman, with a face and a manner that are supremely self-confident yet comforting enough to put a frightened child at ease; her smile comes from deep in her heart. Her fingers are small and nimble, appropriate for her small patients. Other surgeons who've watched her work tell her she has "good hands," and indeed, they are especially strong. Wehby could be a good arm-wrestler.

When Wehby arrived in Portland, she was the first pediatric neurosurgeon in the area to use an innovative procedure to help children with bowel and bladder incontinence. Her technique, involving a subtle spinal cord operation, produced improvement in ninety-five percent of the cases. But some local doctors, the old guard, were skeptical: not only was the technique as yet untried in Portland, but the doctor was young. And a woman. Wehby heard the whispers from the tight-knit medical community. Whispers are something she's dealt with her entire career. A woman doesn't easily become a surgeon, especially a pediatric neurosurgeon. She was the first woman admitted to the grueling seven-year neurosurgical residency program at UCLA's medical school. She has a thick skin. And for her, the only critics who matter, the ones who guide every decision she makes, are her patients and their parents.

Wehby's car climbs onto the ramp leading to the Fremont Bridge. As she drives, she sees her second home—Emanuel Hospital, the region's preeminent children's hospital. She parks her car in a nearly empty garage and enters the hospital through a basement door. In a soft southern accent that's disarmingly friendly, she offers greetings to anyone she encounters: a fellow surgeon, a receptionist, the janitor who rides with her to the third floor. Both the important and those invisible to every other doctor get an honest "Good morning" from Wehby, who remembers her mother's admonition to always be nice to the nurses. She calls people "hon," and likes to touch them to make a point. Her eyes, as much as her voice, reveal what she's thinking. They can flash and harden, and tell the world that she's as tough as the most ornery old surgeon, demanding excellence and silencing the operating room without a word. She can look into a mother's eyes and let her know she understands her pain and fear. And when her eyes soften, when she stops being just a surgeon, she wins the trust of frightened children; they believe this woman will protect them.

Wehby unlocks the door to Microneurosurgical Consultants, the practice in which she's a partner. She's the only woman, recruited in 1997 by doctors she calls "the boys," an experienced group of neurosurgeons whose patients are adults. What attracted her to Portland was the chance to be the pediatric neurosurgeon for the group, a plum job usually reserved for a university professor.

At the front desk she stops to check her schedule, which is taped to the counter. She walks to her office and pulls the CAT scan showing the head of the baby girl whose face she will reconfigure. She's ready, as always, for the operating room.

In the preop waiting room, she sees the patient, with her parents. The mother, as might be expected, seems nervous.

Wehby walks over and greets the family.

"Are you ready?" the mother asks.

Wehby smiles. She takes care of every baby as if the child were her own. Although she doesn't let it show, it irritates her when parents ask her: "What would you do if it were your child?" Every decision she makes, she makes as if it *were* one of her kids.

"Yes, I'm ready," she says. "Once we start, I'll have someone check with you every hour to keep you updated," she tells the parents.

The mother nods. "How are you doing?" she asks Wehby. "Did you sleep okay?"

"I'm doing great," the doctor answers. "But I should be asking you that. Listen, don't worry."

But Wehby herself will worry.

Although she's known for her speed—some days completing four procedures before noon—Wehby is considered the most careful pediatric neurosurgeon ever to pick up a scalpel at Emanuel. Her cases rarely have complications. When she was a resident, she attended every mortality and morbidity meeting and listened as experienced surgeons analyzed cases in which patients died. Her memory is excellent, and she remembers all the complications she's heard about, and before she makes the first incision contemplates ways to avoid them. For her, the patient is not a case or a conquest. The patient is an individual, and someone's child.

Wehby washes her hands at the scrub sink. She pushes open the swinging doors to the operating room with her hip. A nurse hands her a towel for her hands, then helps her into her surgical gown and gloves; she already has a cap on. She looks at the sleeping baby. An anesthesiologist is monitoring her blood pressure and vital signs.

"Do we have the blood here?" she asks the anesthesiologist. As friendly as she is, Wehby expects a high level of confidence and competence from those who assist her. During one operation, a nurse told her that the certain-size tool she requested was not available. Other surgeons would simply have made another quarter-inch incision. But Wehby laid into the nurse—who was a friend—and said that if she had to make another incision, she was going to tell the child's parents that it was the nurse's fault. In the end, she figured a way to avoid the second incision. The anesthesiologist nods.

She sits beside the operating table, next to her partner on the case, Dr. Michael Wheatley. With purple markers the doctors draw lines on the baby's scalp, to guide their incisions.

Wehby uses a razor to shave the baby's scalp. She shakes the razor, depositing the curly brown tufts into a plastic bag that a nurse will later give to the mother as a souvenir.

"Baby's first haircut," she tells the surgical nurse, "and I know Mom will want the hair. Who'd have thought the first haircut would be in an operating room?"

She looks at the purple hair and laughs.

"Mom's going to take one look at that, and wonder what's going on," she says. "We can tell her that's what her daughter's hair will look like when she's a teenager. Isn't that when they all start dyeing their hair these days?"

She gently pulls the baby's scalp, measures, and continues to cut.

"I never did anything like that," she tells the nurse. "Mama said we were good kids."

Childhood memories bring a smile to Wehby's face, make her eyes crinkle—the only feature showing when she wears a surgical mask. There are moments when she feels her grandfather's spirit beside her in the operating room, carefully watching over her as she embarks on the toughest of cases. She was born and raised in Nashville. Her father was an accountant, her mother a registered nurse who gave up her career to stay home with the couple's four children. Early on they knew that Monica, their third child, was different. At age six, she carried on adult-level conversations with her father during weekend drives to the countryside to visit the farm where her mother grew up. Her older brother and sister turned to her for advice. She was captain of her high school cheerleading team, played guitar in a folk group that performed regularly at Sunday Mass, and was elected president of every club she joined. Her

success, though, never came at the expense of others. She had no en-
emies. In her high school yearbook she was voted "Most Popular,"
"Best All Around," and "Friendliest." She liked science and animals,
and after abandoning her girlhood dream of being a ballerina, she
considered becoming a veterinarian. Her father wanted at least one
of his children to be a doctor, passing down the unfulfilled dream of
his own father, an immigrant who had moved to the United States
from Lebanon to make a better life for his family. Her parents di-
vorced when she was in high school. Monica took the news in stride,
setting her sights on leaving Tennessee and becoming a doctor.
When she left home, her father predicted that one day she'd be a
brain surgeon.

She was good with her hands (her grandmother passed down
the skills to knit and crochet, and her mother taught her to embroi-
der) and rotated through the surgical subspecialties. She considered
plastic surgery, but felt she'd end up a cosmetician, helping people
who simply wanted to look better. What intrigued her was the func-
tional side of plastic surgery—doing a nerve graft to make a hand
work correctly, for instance. She looked to neurosurgery, surgery on
the brain and spine, but thought it would require remarkable talents
beyond her abilities. She learned otherwise.

Wehby extends her hand, never taking her eyes off the patient.
The surgical nurse firmly places a scalpel in her right palm. Wehby
begins cutting, following the purple lines, soaking up the baby's
blood with a sponge.

Once the baby's scalp is loose, Wehby calls for the Midas Rex
drill, an air-driven device that allows her to bore holes in the skull. A
whine fills the room, and there's the faint scent that accompanies a
dentist's drilling. Wehby drills, probes, and breaks off pieces of the
skull, which are placed in a container filled with antibacterial solution. Slowly, she separates the bone from the dura, or dura mater, the

leatherlike encasement for the brain. She sees the draining vein pulsing, the most delicate element here. She has to remove the bone from the dura without damaging that vein. Everything rides on her touch and judgment. A big piece of bone is stuck directly over the vein. Carefully, she inserts probes between the dura and the bone, and levers the bone free. She pushes, tests, then pushes again.

"Thank you, Jesus," she sighs.

The problem with the baby's skull occurred in the womb. The plates that form the skull closed too early, leaving the girl with a pointed head and eyes too close together. Wehby and Wheatley plan to reshape the girl's forehead, flatten it, and remodel the bones surrounding the eyes. The skin has been peeled back from the baby's face, and covers her eyes and nose. Wehby pulls the flap back onto the dura, and thinks about what must be done to make this little girl look pretty, normal. This is one of the most rewarding parts of Wehby's job—changing a life. She stands and stretches before the next stage begins.

Over time, even the most careful orthopedic surgeon may begin to take an ankle joint for granted. Wehby never fails to look at the brain and be amazed: it's the most interesting organ in the body. And the most treacherous. With most other organs, the surgeon can fix a mistake. Not so with the brain. Cut too much of the surrounding tissue when removing a tumor, for example, and the patient loses brain function. Make another mistake, and the patient can die.

Wehby spent seven years as a resident at UCLA's medical school, learning how to be a neurosurgeon, and an additional eighteen months as a fellow—an elite honor—at Primary Children's Medical Center in Salt Lake City. No other surgical field requires such lengthy training. What everyone drilled into Wehby was that there's nothing routine about pediatric surgery. The center, the thirteenth-largest freestanding pediatric hospital in the nation, serves patients from four surrounding states. With that volume, Wehby operated continuously and saw every imaginable case. She also learned something else: how to control her emotions. A boyfriend got mad at her, complaining that nothing ever upset her. Even her husband—an anesthesiologist who works part-time—tells her that she thinks more like a man than a woman.

With so much at stake, Wehby must bury her emotions. Pediatric neurosurgery is often thought to be the most depressing of specialties. Medical students often complete a rotation and vow never to do it again. Bad news and unpredictable outcomes, along with the other intense pressures of dealing with young lives, can kill a pediatric neurosurgeon's spirit. And pediatric neurosurgeons must think not only of their patients, but also of the worried parents, who pepper them with questions and sometimes harbor doubts.

Wehby sits on a stool to the right of the baby's head. Wheatley stands beside her. Using pieces of the baby's skull, they shape a new forehead. They cut, hold the pieces together, and imagine what they will look like under the skin. Although she chats with the nurses, Wehby never lets her mind wander from the case. She's learned that surgeons get into trouble when they think they are better than they actually are. Doubts, she's come to believe, are a good thing, as important to a surgeon as is confidence.

"How does this look?" she asks Wheatley as she holds up a section of bone. He nods. "This is my favorite part of the surgery. It's art and sculpture. It's low-stress, and you get immediate gratification."

They screw the pieces of skull into high-tech plastic that costs $1,200 a sheet, to form a flat forehead. Holding everything together is glue that costs $500 a gram. Wehby will fill in the gaps between the skull and the plastic sheet with the same glue. In time, the adhesive will harden and grow new bone, and the screws will dissolve.

With her fingers, Wehby continues shaping the skull. Then she uses a tool to snap part of the girl's skull. Green-twig fractures, these snapping breaks are called, because they sound as if small twigs were being broken. The fractures stop the flow of blood and actually help speed reconstruction.

Wehby folds the skin down over her work. She makes sure the baby's face is symmetrical.

"She looks good. Beautiful, if I do say so myself."

But Wehby wants others' opinions. She asks everyone in the room to look at the baby's face, from all angles.

"Does her forehead look normal? Anything wrong, before we close?"

Everyone thinks the child looks great. Wehby, though, isn't satisfied. She cleans up the right side of the head, near the temple, smoothing glue onto the skull. She folds the baby's skin flap back into place. She polls the room once more.

"Anything wrong? Anyone?"

The room is silent.

"Okay," Wehby says, "Let's close and get the hell out of here."


They close up quickly. More than five hours have passed since Wehby entered the operating room. She walks to an alcove in the room and telephones her office.

"You can bring the kids in a little earlier," Wehby tells her assistant, Lora Beth Nava. As she listens to Nava, she jots notes about the surgery in the patient's report.

"He died?" Wehby asks. She stops writing. "At the hospice?

Everyone was there? Let me know the time of the funeral. I'm glad I told them it was a matter of days."

The patient was a five-year-old boy who fell and hit his head while ice-skating. Although he had no obvious injuries, he complained to his parents, and as a precaution they took him to the hospital's emergency room. A routine scan looked suspicious, and the emergency room contacted Wehby. She too thought the scan looked suspicious, and scheduled him for surgery. When she opened the boy's head, she discovered an inoperable brain-stem tumor. And the cancer had wound its way down the boy's spinal cord—as extensive a case as she had ever seen. There was nothing she could do. The child had just months to live. She left the operating room to pass on the grim news to the boy's parents. She saw them huddled with friends. Wehby asked a nurse to pull the parents aside and take them to a private room where she could speak with them.

She has steeled herself to never cry in front of parents. Sometimes she fails. She wants them to know she cares, but they also must believe that their neurosurgeon is thinking clearly.

She leaves the operating room, to find the parents of the nine-month-old.

"It went well," she tells them. "She looks beautiful."

The mother gives Wehby a hug.

"You can go see her in a while," Wehby says. "Her face will look a little poofy, but everything's fine. She's going to look just great."

Wehby smiles and turns down the hall, then goes to her office. Her assistant is completing the next day's schedule. Tomorrow Wehby will see sixteen patients. Today she has only six.

As tired as she is at the end of the day, Wehby goes to visit the nine-month-old. The grandmother and another relative have been watching the child. Wehby moves quietly to the side of the crib and places her hand gently on the child's stomach.

"Precious baby," she whispers. "You did well today."

She turns to the grandmother. "Has she been awake, kicking and moving?"

"Oh, yes."

"Good," Wehby says.

"Her parents are thrilled," the grandmother says. "Her father started crying when he saw her. You know, he's had to keep all those emotions inside. They just had to come out."

"I know the feeling," Wehby says.

Dr. Monica Wehby arrives home just before eight p.m.—today is a little shorter than average. She goes to her children in the kitchen.

She gives each of them a hug. They've already eaten dinner and want her to read to them. They hand her a book. She turns to the first page, fights a yawn.

"One day . . ."

Monica Wehby is home. Soon, morning will return and Dr. Monica Wehby with it.

**17** Sam Lightner heard his father walk into the room, but didn't turn his head. It hurt to do anything but look straight ahead. His father sat on the sofa and handed Sam the local newspaper. Months before, the boy had agreed to tell the story of his life.

"Here it is, Sam. Check it out."

Sam glanced at the front page. There was a picture of him in his Boy Scout uniform. The picture was huge.

"What do you think?" his mother asked.

Sam started to read the first paragraph. He couldn't concentrate. He skimmed, he wandered. He just didn't care. He looked at the other pictures, then tossed the newspaper to the floor.

His mother picked it up and began reading the story aloud. Sam nodded at the parts he thought were good. But he was tired. He told his mother to finish reading it to him later. Now he just wanted to watch television.

Two days later, on October 3, 2000, Sam was again too sick to go to school. By now he had missed two weeks, and he worried about falling behind. Teachers had sent homework, but he hadn't been able to focus. During the week, his locker buddy called to say that everyone at Grant was talking about the newspaper story. Sam was the most popular boy in school. Even more popular than the high school's star quarterback. Sam laughed at that one.

His days had been spent in isolation. In the morning his parents left for work, Emily and Nathan for school. Debbie worried about him, but he said he was fine. He was just sick to his stomach. Still, she called twice a day to check on him.

He would sit on the sofa in the basement, Maggie the dog curled up next to him. He would watch television until he was bored. Then he'd sit in front of the computer and play games or go on-line.

Today he noticed that walking just a few feet was tricky. He stood up and fell back on the sofa. Maybe his legs were stiff from sitting for so long. He got up again and felt wobbly. He held on to the back of a chair until he could take three steps, then sit down and play on the computer.

The day passed slowly. He was tired, but couldn't sleep. When he lay down, he felt nauseated. He sat up and the feeling passed. He held his head perfectly still. Sitting like a statue made it bearable. He moved his head from side to side, testing his body, trying to figure out what was wrong. That felt okay. Just a little dizzy.

He lay his head back on the sofa cushion. There. It felt as if something were pushing deep inside his brain. It didn't hurt, only felt strange.

Debbie Lightner arrived home on the afternoon of October 3 wondering what her family might want for dinner. And what would Sam want? He hadn't been feeling well, but last night he had eaten handfuls of Oreos. Maybe her son the medical mystery was on the mend.

She opened the car door and stepped into the sun. Like everyone in Portland, she was enjoying these days that seemed to want to fool people into thinking the rainy season wasn't approaching. She entered the house through the back door, set her purse on the kitchen table, and went to change. Emily had said she'd be at a friend's house. Nathan was in the living room. She wondered how Sam's day had gone since she'd called.

"Sam?" she called.

"He's in the basement," Nathan told her.

She went downstairs. Sam sat on the sofa, the dog next to him. On the other side was a pan Sam could use if he had to throw up.

"How are you feeling?" Debbie asked.

He shook his head.

"Oh, Sam. What are we going to do?"

He shrugged and petted the dog. He had no answers. All he knew was that he was tired and dizzy, and his head ached.

Debbie looked at his face, drained of color, and his waxy skin. She felt his forehead. No fever, but his one good eye had lost its sparkle. She went to the kitchen and reached for the telephone.

The medical specialists she'd taken Sam to see hadn't been able to find anything wrong with him. "Maybe an ear infection." "Maybe a touch of the flu." "Maybe just some rest." All she'd heard was a bunch of maybes. No one knew for sure what was going on with her son. But she had to do something for him.

She called Dr. Campbell, but he wasn't in. Next she called the family's pediatrician. Debbie told the receptionist it was important that Dr. Davis see her son as soon as possible. She was told to bring Sam in right away.

From the top of the basement stairs she called for Sam to get ready.

There was no answer.

She went down the stairs. "Sam," she said, "let's go."

Sam set the dog on the floor and pushed himself off the sofa. He was surprised at how hard he had to work to make his legs do what he wanted them to do. As he tried to stand he teetered and fell back onto the sofa. His feet trembled. He looked at them moving, kicking, as if he were having a seizure. This was like watching someone else's body. He was scared.

"It's okay," Debbie said. She reached under his arms and helped him stand, then slowly accompanied him upstairs.

In the kitchen, he felt his body tugged to the left, as if someone were pulling him by a rope tied around his waist. He fought the pull and concentrated, trying to force his body to do what he wanted it to do.

Nathan ran outside and opened the car doors. Sam and Debbie walked outside. When she let go of Sam's arm to lock the door of the house, he started walking in a circle on the driveway.

"Sam," she warned, "don't move. You're going to fall."

Sam wanted to stop. He concentrated, harder than ever. He was fighting his brain for control of his body.

He lost. He turned in a circle.

Sam felt his mother's hand on his shoulder. She steadied him. He looked down at the driveway, taking step after careful step until he was beside the car. He slumped into the front seat, exhausted.

———

Sam looked up when the door opened, but he couldn't even manage a wave to Dr. Davis. He'd known Davis since he was about five. Sam came to him for his well-baby checkups, and when he needed forms filled out for camp. He usually asked Sam about school or talked about how the Blazers were doing in the NBA standings.

"So what's the problem?" Davis asked. Sam couldn't speak. He couldn't smile.

"You're our third stop." Debbie explained how they had seen Campbell and the ear, nose, and throat specialist.

"He throws up, and then he gets a little better," Debbie said. "He's dizzy and he has trouble controlling his legs. Something isn't right, but no one can find anything wrong with him."

Davis sat on a stool close to Sam. He listened to Sam's heart with a stethoscope. He peered down his throat, checked for ear infection, and took his temperature. Everything normal. And yet Sam looked terrible.

"He can't eat," Debbie said. "He can't keep anything down but water."

"Tell me about the dizziness," Davis asked Debbie. "And these headaches."

"It's been going on for at least two weeks," Debbie said. "Does that sound right, Sam?"

All the talk about headaches and throwing up made Sam feel worse. He forced himself to nod.

"Oh, and he has trouble with his left arm," Debbie said.

"Let me see you move your arm for me," Davis instructed.

Sam couldn't lift his arm. He tried again.

"I don't want to worry you," Davis said. "But I think we need to know what's going on inside his head. I want you to take him to the hospital."

Davis left the room and called Northwest Magnetic Imaging Center, a private lab within Emanuel Hospital. "I'm going to be sending a patient who needs to be seen right away," he told the telephone receptionist.

When Debbie and Sam arrived at Emanuel, technicians were waiting. The procedure would take at least an hour, and Sam would have to be lightly sedated. If he moved during the scan, a technician explained, the films of his brain would appear blurry. The technicians pushed Sam to the imaging room. Debbie found a phone to call David.

Technicians had Sam lie on the gantry, his head immobilized. Red laser lines created a holograph that divided his face into sectors; in a different setting, he'd look like a rock star. His head became, in effect, a loaf of bread about to be sliced photographically into twenty pictures, each showing a five-millimeter section of his brain.

The scan over, a technician led Debbie back to her son, who was lying on a gurney.

"He's having a bit of a hard time waking up," the technician said.

"Sam," Debbie called. "Sam."

The room was dimly lit. Maybe he was just asleep.

"Sam, wake up. How are you?"

The technician approached Debbie and motioned to her. "I think we found hydrocephalus," he said.

"What's that?" Debbie asked. /

"I'm going to have your pediatrician talk with you," he said.

"Can I take my son home?"

"No, he won't be leaving here tonight."

Sam stirred, and Debbie wanted to make sure he wasn't scared.

"Sam," she said, "we have to stay here. They're going to fix the problem and then you can go home."

After the films were developed, they were studied by a radiologist, who called Dr. Davis. Davis, in turn, called Debbie, who was still waiting in the Imaging Center.

The technician waved to Debbie with the telephone.

"Sam has a buildup of fluid in his brain," Davis told her. He explained that spinal fluid, produced in the brain, drains into ventricles, which send the fluid through channels that cut through the brain stem. These empty into the spinal cord, where the fluid circulates and is absorbed into the body. In Sam's case, some pressure on those channels had trapped the fluid in the brain. That pressure made Sam feel nauseated and dizzy.

"Is it serious?" Debbie asked.

"Yes," Davis said. "We have to relieve the pressure. That's the job of a pediatric neurosurgeon. Someone will have to go into his brain."

The brain? Debbie felt her heart race. Brain surgery? The words frightened her. Davis assured her that all would be well. Putting in a brain shunt was a routine procedure.

"You have a choice," Davis said. "There's a pediatric neurosurgeon at the university hospital. He's a good one. Or you can stay at Emanuel."

Hours before, she was trying to figure out dinner. Now Debbie Lightner was being asked to select a brain surgeon for her fourteen-year-old son. Davis awaited her answer.

"I want to stay here."

"Okay," Davis said. "You got Wehby."

**18** Dr. Wehby had just arrived home after another hectic day. She was tired, and on call all week, meaning she had to respond to any hospital emergency involving a child with a head or spinal injury.

Today she'd seen patients during clinic, and then was summoned to an operating room to install a shunt in the head of a boy with a brain tumor. Some pediatric neurosurgeons, since retired, routinely took up to two hours for brain shunts, commonly used to relieve pressure in the brain by draining fluid. Wehby regularly completed hers in thirty minutes, which meant less chance of infection. At times Wehby felt as if she were something of a shunt dumping ground. If they were easy, someone else did them. But the moment they got confusing, they ended up on her watch. The next day's schedule promised to be especially grueling. She had to be at the hospital by seven-thirty for a complex spinal cord operation expected to last at least five hours.

Though it was only eight p.m., she imagined how wonderful it would feel to walk upstairs, crawl into bed, and drift off to sleep. What she relished wasn't so much the sleep as the chance not to have to think, and not to have to think for other people—patients and their parents, other doctors, nurses. At the very least, she hoped that her kids would sleep through the night. The chances of that happening, however, were about as slim as her going to bed soon.

The four kids heard the back door open and ran to greet their mother. She stepped over toys scattered on the floor and picked up her youngest son. She was carrying him into the kitchen when the telephone rang. The hospital operator was on the line, and she asked Wehby to hold for an incoming call. Wehby stood waiting, her kids clamoring for her full attention.

"Hello, Monica?"

Wehby recognized Steve Davis's voice. It was never good news when a pediatrician called a neurosurgeon after hours. The pediatrician wasn't asking for advice about an ear infection.

"You know that boy Sam Lightner?" Davis asked her after they had caught up with each other. "Maybe you saw the article about him in the paper over the weekend."

Yes, Wehby had seen the story on him. She hadn't read it all, but she had looked at the pictures, and had heard about his vascular malformation. And tonight, as she was leaving the hospital, she told Davis, she thought she had seen him in the Imaging Center waiting room. She'd assumed he was having a postoperative scan on the remains of the malformation that clung to the left side of his face. Surgeons had been talking about the series of stories all week, their feathers ruffled because the kid had gone to the *great* Boston Children's Hospital for what seemed to be a particularly dangerous operation, one, they sarcastically remarked, that was beyond the reach of *simple* Portland surgeons. Wehby had been tempted to stop, since kids who needed scans usually had problems that brought them to her office. But the boy wasn't her patient.

"He had a scan," Davis said, "but it's not for postop. After looking at the films, they think it might be hydrocephalus. His ventricles look big."

Wehby set her son on the floor. By now the other children had returned to playing.

"Was there transependymal flow?" she asked.

Davis didn't know. That was a question only an expert could answer.

"How bad is he?"

"He doesn't look good," Davis said. "He's at the hospital, but he hasn't been admitted yet."

Wehby thanked Davis, hung up, and called the Imaging Center, hoping there was still someone on duty at this hour. Luckily there was.

"Is it acute?" she asked the radiologist who had read Sam's films.

"I don't know. The draining ventricles are big, but this boy's anatomy is skewed. He has naturally big ventricles."

Wehby couldn't believe this news. Wednesday was her big operating day. She hadn't eaten. Her kids wanted her to play with them and read to them. They wanted her to tuck them into bed and sit with them while they fell asleep. Sometimes it seemed to Wehby that she neglected her own children. Every other child depended on her. And by necessity those children had to come first. She believed that only a fellow surgeon could truly understand the pressure and responsibility she felt when a parent entrusted a child to her, said good-bye in the pre-surgery waiting room, then watched her disappear down the hall and through the doors that led to the operating room.

As she stood in her home office surrounded by toys and dirty clothes, the radiologist answering her questions, she thought hard about this case. Wehby had never met this Lightner boy or his family. He wasn't her patient. And his ventricles *might* just be big by nature. Maybe it could wait until morning. She was hungry, and wanted to spend some time with her kids.

But then fluid on the brain was dangerous. Parents always panicked when Wehby uttered the word "tumor." But a steady buildup of fluid and pressure was potentially more dangerous—a kid could die in a matter of hours. Too much pressure, and this boy's brain would be shoved up against the unforgiving wall of the skull.

Despite her quiet and unshakable confidence in the operating room, Wehby was a worrier. While many doctors were efficient and logical to the point of seeming devoid of emotion, Wehby thought constantly about her patients and her decisions. Even though she was recognized as one of the top surgeons at Emanuel, she always wondered whether she was good enough, whether she'd done enough for the kids under her care, looked at enough scans or lingered enough when she made rounds.

When surgery was successful, she felt the thrill of telling nervous parents in the waiting room that all was well. But she was also there for the low, when she brought bad news, when parents most needed her support. In the four years she'd been at Emanuel, only a handful of people had seen her shed a tear. When she cried, it was when she was alone. She attended the funerals of patients who had died, offering words of comfort to parents and sometimes speaking to those gathered. She once left a note, "Best friends, Love, Monica," at the coffin of a thirteen-year-old girl. She believed some of these children—angels, she called them—hovered over her, watching her as she operated. These angels were there too for the children Wehby knew would die, those with the inoperable tumors. Her surgical skills were world-class. Yet as difficult as they were, those techniques could be learned and honed over the years by any number of surgeons. That wasn't what made Wehby a great surgeon. The secret was her heart. And a good heart was something that couldn't be taught. Wehby's heart told her that if she didn't go to the hospital for a look at the scans, she'd be up all night second-guessing herself.

"Okay," Wehby told the radiologist. "I'm coming in."

She hung up and told her husband that she had to return to the hospital.

"But I'll be right back," she said. "I won't have to do anything tonight."

Wehby carried the scans to the view box in the scanner room and flipped on the lights. Black areas showed Sam's ventricles, two on top of the brain that emptied into a third, which led to a fourth ventricle. The ventricles were huge, and backed up with spinal fluid; the cerebellum was being squeezed. Davis had told her about the boy's headaches and dizziness, and this was the reason. Wehby figured that the problem was subacute, that it had been building gradually for weeks, until his brain could no longer tolerate the pressure.

She would have to drain off the excess spinal fluids. She could use an external shunt, which would allow her to monitor the fluid as it drained off, or a standard internal shunt, which would lead from the ventricles into Sam's abdominal cavity, in which case the fluids would be absorbed by the body.

She left the scanner room and proceeded to the ward where Sam and Debbie Lightner waited. By now Sam had been admitted to the hospital.

Wehby explained the situation to Debbie. "I do shunts all the time," she said. "It's not a difficult procedure. It's the appendectomy of my field, and it needs to be done."

She waited to be peppered with questions.

Debbie had just one: "So you're going to do this tonight?"

"Yes."

"I'd like to call my husband."

"You can call him," Wehby said. "But I'm not waiting for him to get here. I'm going right now."

Debbie nodded. "Sam," she said, "I'm going to call Dad. This doctor's going to make you feel better." She leaned over and kissed her son.

He felt so groggy. He just wanted to go home. There was no real pain in his head anymore. He heard this doctor ask him something, and he tried to think through the fog surrounding him. As if from a distance, he heard the doctor ask him to move his hand. He concentrated. He moved it. Or it felt like he did. But the doctor was frowning. She asked him to move his leg. He tried his best. Yet with each passing minute, he felt like he was losing control of his arms and legs. Even his fingers. The doctor asked him to hold up three. He wasn't sure if he was doing as she requested. He just wanted to sleep.

Wehby was troubled. The boy was also suffering from apnea, pauses in his breathing. He was in worse shape than the scans indicated. The ability to breathe is one of the last functions a person loses. If Davis hadn't sent him to the hospital tonight, Sam might have died.

David Lightner had rushed to the hospital, and now he sprinted down the hall. Wehby introduced herself. She told the Lightners they could accompany Sam when attendants brought him from his room to the operating room in the basement. There was a waiting room nearby; it would be empty at this time of night.

"Don't worry," she told the Lightners before heading to the basement herself. "I'll be done with this in thirty minutes."

A surgical team was assembled and ready when she reached the operating room. Soon after, a nurse notified Wehby that Sam had arrived. His bed was in the hall in front of the control desk. The doctor took Sam's hand in hers, smiling at him and walking alongside as his bed was pushed down the hall.

"Don't worry, Sam," she said. "Everything will be fine."

The bed was wheeled into position under surgical lights that had yet to be activated. The anesthesiologist ran lines into Sam, readying him for sleep. Wehby held Sam's hand as he dozed off. She remembered the first time she herself had to go under the knife. She'd been in medical school. Even though she knew the surgeon was good, she was scared. A kind nurse had stood by her bed, holding her hand, comforting her, until she fell asleep. Since then, Wehby vowed to be there for her patients at that moment. She'd be there to look them in the eye as they drifted off to sleep, to let them know that Dr. Monica Wehby—the surgeon in pearls—would watch over them, care for them, be there when they woke up. Wehby leaned over the bed.

"It's okay, Sam. I'm here."

And then the boy was out.

Wehby gently tucked Sam's hand next to his frail body. She examined his head. She usually avoided placing a shunt on the patient's dominant brain hemisphere. In a right-handed person, that would be the left. If there was a problem with the shunt, the dominant hemisphere wouldn't be damaged. It was fortunate that Sam was right-handed, because the left side of his head was laden with problems from the vascular malfunction. Wehby understood why Portland surgeons had turned this kid away. She wondered what had made the surgeons in Boston believe they could help him.

Wehby ordered that the operating table be turned so that Sam's head would be closer to where she liked to stand. She stuck a rolled towel under his right shoulder to raise it and create a straight pathway for the shunt line from his head to his abdomen. With her fingers she felt for the sutures in his skull, and for the spot where she would stick a four-inch catheter needle, plunging it through brain matter into the ventricle. She'd be guided by experience and touch. The brain would "talk" to her: with its Jell-O consistency, it would resist when she shoved in the catheter. When there was no more resistance, she'd know the catheter had popped into the ventricle lake. She found the spot where she wanted to cut, shaved a small clearing in Sam's hair, and marked it in purple. She injected his scalp with an anesthetic to constrict the blood vessels and lessen the chance of bleeding. Then she marked another spot in purple on his abdomen.

She left the room to scrub up while the nurses finished prepping Sam. They taped his eyes shut, covered his body with blue sheets, and attached towels to his head. The only areas left exposed were those where Wehby would cut: the spot on his head, just behind his right ear, and the spot on his abdomen. Tubing between those two spots would allow the fluid to flow out of his brain.

As simple as the shunting process sounds, there were possible complications that Wehby was aware of, among them bleeding, infection, and too quick a release in pressure in the brain, which would force it out through the base of the skull.

Wehby moved quickly into the operating room, where a nurse helped her into surgical garb. An incision on the head, then the Midas Rex drill into Sam's skull. She put wax around the drilled hole to keep blood from dripping into his brain when she passed the

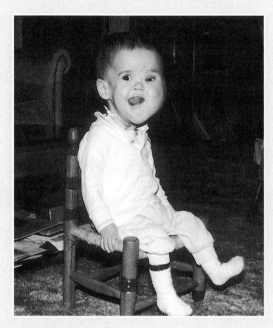

February 1987.
Sam Lightner is
sixteen months old.
*(Lightner family)*

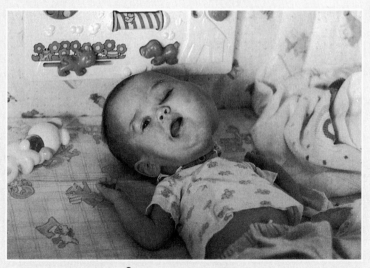

Sam at eleven months.
*(Lightner family)*

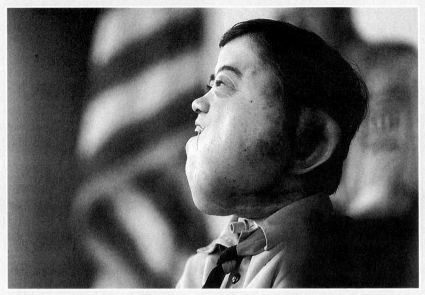

Sam at a Boy Scouts meeting. On troop outings, while other boys carry extra clothes and gear in their knapsacks, Sam takes along a portable suction device to clear his tracheostomy. (© *Benjamin Brink* / THE OREGONIAN)

On the Internet, Sam is just another screen name in a chat room, where his words speak for themselves, independent of his distorted voice and his appearance. (© *Benjamin Brink* / THE OREGONIAN)

The Lightner family on their front porch.
(© *Benjamin Brink* / THE OREGONIAN)

Sam volunteers to answer a question posed during a hallway study session as he and fellow Gregory Heights students prepare for a history test.
(© *Benjamin Brink* / THE OREGONIAN)

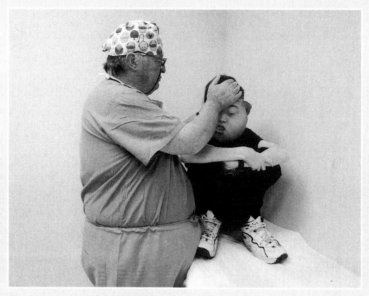

Dr. Tim Campbell, the Portland surgeon who operated on Sam shortly after his birth, encounters him again as a fourteen-year-old. (© *Benjamin Brink* / THE OREGONIAN)

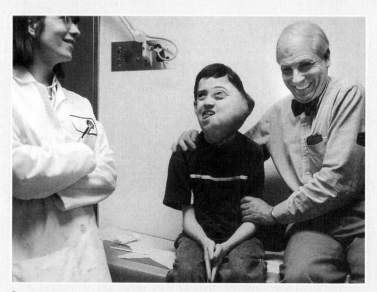

Dr. Jennifer Marler (left) is Sam's persistent advocate, urging her colleagues to bring him to Boston. There, Dr. John Mulliken meets him for the first time. (© *Benjamin Brink* / THE OREGONIAN)

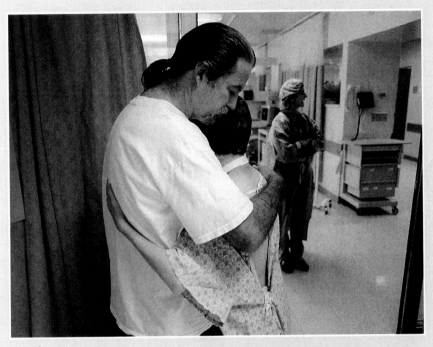

At Boston Children's Hospital, David Lightner wraps his arms around
his son as a nurse waits to accompany Sam to the operating room.
(© *Benjamin Brink* / THE OREGONIAN)

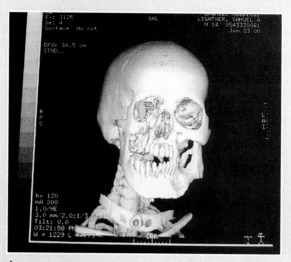

A three-dimensional CAT scan reveals the extent of the bone deformity beneath the mass on Sam's face. (© *Benjamin Brink* / The Oregonian)

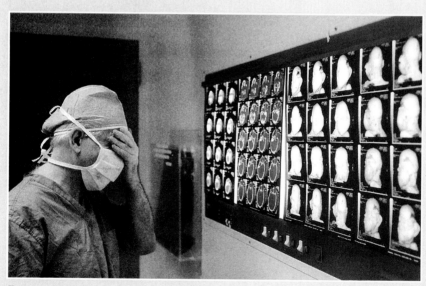

The surgery drags on for hours, and Mulliken, taking a breather in front of an array of Sam's CAT scans, feels frustrated and exhausted. (© *Benjamin Brink* / The Oregonian)

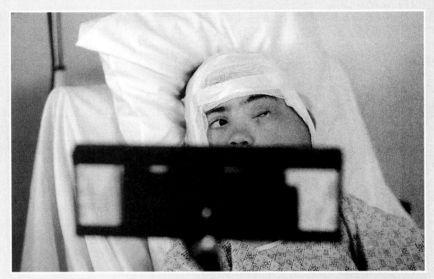

After surgery, Sam communicates by pressing programmed keys on a small computer suspended in front of him. He presses one key to say "I hurt."
(© *Benjamin Brink* / The Oregonian)

Dr. Monica Wehby.
(© *2002 Julie Keefe*)

Sam and David, on Sam's first day of high school.
(Lightner family)

catheter. In less than thirty seconds, the drill cut through the skull. Wehby punctured the dura with the catheter and guided it to the ventricle.

A spurt of clear fluid shot out of the catheter. Wehby capped it. She didn't want to decompress the brain suddenly. She slid the shunt passer, a hollow plastic tube, through the hole in Sam's head and guided it through the tissue between scalp and skull. She made an incision at the ear and pushed twice, and the passer poked free. She fed the shunt through the passer, pulled out the passer and tossed it aside. Next she reached for what the nurses called the "tool of death."

This was a metal rod about two feet long, and about as thick as a pencil, contained within a plastic sheath. That sheath—it resembled a plastic straw—would run from Sam's ear to his navel and allow Wehby to feed a drainage line under his skin. She bent one end of the rod toward the ceiling so it wouldn't push into Sam's body. She slid the rod into the hole behind Sam's ear and leaned into the tool, shoving and straining. Slowly Sam's body gave way. She could see the rod ripple along under his skin. When it reached his navel, she made an incision, and the rod poked through his skin. She removed the metal rod, leaving behind the plastic sheath. After feeding the drainage line through, she pulled out the sheath. Wehby called for a trocar, which would allow her to punch through Sam's skin directly into his abdominal cavity. She had to be careful not to hit his bladder or bowel; she wanted only the fluid sac where the bowel floated.

She returned to Sam's skull and hooked up the shunt. Gradually the fluid began to flow from the ventricle, down the plastic tubing in Sam's body, to his abdomen. The shunt regulated the flow, maintaining a steady rate of discharge, letting the brain adjust to the drainage.

Wehby closed the incisions. The anesthesiologist began bringing Sam up. When he was awake, he was lifted from the operating table to his bed and then wheeled out of the room.

Wehby sat on a stool and completed her paperwork. She glanced at the clock on the wall: one-forty a.m. The shunt, she reflected, had been a breeze.

**19** Dr. Wehby briefed the Lightners in the waiting room. They had decided to stay at the hospital to be with Sam. She planned to stick around long enough to check on him in the recovery room, to make sure all was well. She talked to a nurse about whether to send Sam back to the ward or admit him to Pediatric Intensive Care. The nurse said Sam looked great—he was awake, his vital signs were fine, and he was breathing on his own—and recommended the ward. Okay, Wehby said, send him to the ward. She thanked the recovery room nurses, picked up her purse at the control desk, and left the hospital.

As she drove home, though, Monica Wehby started to worry. Should she have put him in the ICU?

No, he was doing fine.

But still.

These doubts were the part of the job no one saw. She pulled into the garage at home, walked in the back door, and kicked off her surgical clogs. She had to know what was going on with Sam. She called the recovery room.

"How's Sam doing?"

"He's perfect," the nurse told her. "He's following commands and looks great. No sign of apnea. We're going to send him up to the floor now."

"Have the nurses watch him," Wehby said. "If there are any questions, any at all, if he's not perfect, send him to the ICU."

"He's fine."

"Remember, he had apnea," Wehby said. "If there's any problems, get him to the ICU."

"He looks good."

Wehby hung up, checked that the doors were locked, and turned off the lights. She walked upstairs and peeked in the rooms of her sleeping children. She went down the hall and into the bathroom, and slipped out of her surgical scrubs. she removed her contact lenses, washed her face, and brushed her teeth. She slid into bed.

But she was still uneasy. She had that big surgery in a few hours. She'd be tired all day, probably for the rest of the week. And something else gnawed at her. Because Sam had been featured in the newspaper, he was now a high-profile patient, known to hundreds of thousands of readers throughout the region, easily the most prominent patient in any hospital in the Pacific Northwest. People throughout the hospital had been talking about him, his surgery, and his struggle to be accepted as a normal fourteen-year-old.

And now, simply because she'd been on call this week, he'd become her patient and her responsibility. If something had happened to him the week before instead, she'd be home asleep and a partner of hers would be on the hot seat.

She felt she was being dragged into something not of her making. She turned her head to glance at the clock. She shouldn't have done that: two forty-five. She closed her eyes, tried to relax, let her mind drift. She couldn't help herself. She looked at the clock again: three a.m.

Damn it! She had to be in the OR in less than five hours. She needed to sleep. She forced herself to forget about Sam Lightner and the spinal case and surgery. The bed was warm. Then the phone rang, and she sat up in a heartbeat.

"Hello?" Her voice was as clear as if she'd been awake.

"Dr. Wehby?" It was a ward clerk at Emanuel. "They wanted us to call you. Your patient is being coded."

"What?"

Wehby flipped back the blankets and swung her feet onto the floor. She carried the cordless phone across the room, looking for a new set of scrubs. Her husband heard the commotion.

"Now what?" he asked.

"They're coding that kid," she explained. "God damn it, I knew something was going to go wrong."

"They put in a code," the clerk repeated on the phone.

"Give me someone who knows what's going on," Wehby demanded.

The resident came on. "He started to have some respiratory problems. The nurse was worried he wasn't breathing."

"Did you bag him?"

"Yes."

"Did he code?"

"No."

Wehby was frustrated.

"Who else is there?"

"An anesthesiologist."

"Get him."

Wehby put her contacts in.

When the anesthesiologist came on, Wehby recognized the voice of Dr. Paul Rose, whom she'd worked with on numerous cases. Rose too had been on call, required to stay at the hospital for a twenty-four-hour shift. When the code sounded, he'd hurried over.

"What's going on?" Wehby asked.

Rose explained that Sam had stopped breathing and a nurse had coded him, alerting the staff. Because he had a tracheostomy, resuscitating him had been easy. Rose had slipped a resuscitating bag over the trach and squeezed it by hand, in effect breathing for Sam, who was now awake.

"Did his heart rate drop?" Wehby asked.

"No."

"What about his blood pressure?"

"No."

"Is it apnea?"

"Well, Monica, it's more than that."

"I'm on my way in."


Wehby drives as if she were from the East Coast, not from Nashville, Tennessee. On the best days, it takes her about fifteen minutes to get from her house to Emanuel. Tonight, she was in the hospital parking lot in less than ten. On her way into the emergency entrance, she ran into a head-and-neck surgeon just coming out of a trauma case.

"Hey, they're coding your kid," he called out when he spotted Wehby. "I read about him in the paper."

My kid, she thought to herself. Great.

"I know," she said, hustling to the elevator. "I'm on my way up there."

In the Pediatric School-Age Unit, she found Dr. Rose and the Lightners in Sam's room. Debbie explained that she and David had gone to their son's room, planning to spend the night there. Debbie sat in the recliner but couldn't sleep. Sam was moaning and shifting in the bed. She checked on him, tried to soothe him. When she pulled the blankets to cover him, she noticed that his chest was red and blotchy. She asked two nurses to take a look at him.

As they walked into the room, they heard him struggle to breathe. His eyes were closed, as if he were sleeping. The nurses asked him to wake up. He wouldn't stir. Take a deep breath, they called. He didn't respond. One of the nurses hit the blue code button. In seconds, ten other nurses and a resident crowded into the room. Then Rose was called, and used the resuscitating bag to help Sam breathe. He seemed like a balky motor—he would start breathing, labor, and then stop. Rose would get him going and the process would repeat itself.

Wehby stood by Sam's bed. He was awake.

"Sam," she said, "you're going to give me a heart attack."

Wehby said she would send Sam to Pediatric Intensive Care, where nurses would constantly watch him. The news scared the Lightners, but Wehby reassured them that Sam's heart had not stopped and that he had not sustained any damage. Anesthesia, sedation, and pressure on his brain were the likely causes of the apnea. And because of Debbie's sharp eye, the nurses had responded before Sam was in any danger.

"Maybe he had too much anesthesia," she said. "Let's give him some Narcan." The drug would counteract the effects of the anesthesia, effectively flush it out of his system.

The apnea returned. For the next two hours, Wehby stood by Sam's bed, monitoring his vital signs. They were strong, and he would rally, breathing on his own, but then need to be bagged, like a motor requiring help in getting started. At about six in the morning, Wehby noticed that Sam was fading. His body heaved, trying to suck in air. It was a losing battle. She ordered him hooked to a ventilator, which would force oxygen into his lungs.

"He's crapping out on us," Wehby told the nurses.

She leaned over his bed. "Sam," she called. "Sam."

No response. She shook him and applied a sternal rub, grinding her fingers into his chest—a painful procedure neurosurgeons use to gauge a patient's response. Nothing.

"What the hell," Wehby said. "I want him scanned again."

Just after seven—eleven hours after she'd first been called at home—Wehby called the operating room control desk and told the staff to push back the start of her seven-thirty case.

She wanted Sam to have a brain scan in the CAT scan room. An MRI would take too long, and the boy's condition made it too dangerous to subject him to a session at the Magnetic Imaging Center. Even now it took five nurses to walk alongside the bed, monitoring the ventilator and vital signs.

Wehby had Sam brought back to the ICU while she waited for the scans. His parents were seeing him slip away before their eyes. They would yell at him, trying to get him to respond. But he wasn't awake. His eyes were shut tight, and his entire face was swollen; his tongue was growing in size and being pushed out of his mouth.

Two floors below the ICU, Wehby studied the films and saw one thing she most feared—blood.

There was a new problem, something more serious, centered in the posterior fossa, the area of the brain that houses the brain stem and cerebellum. The brain stem is the most critical part of the brain, connecting it to the spinal cord and controlling the neurological functions necessary for survival—breathing, heartbeat, maintenance of blood pressure, swallowing. The cerebellum coordinates motor and mental functions, allowing a person to walk, talk, and eat.

Wehby considered the possibility that the vascular malformation had sprung to life and grown into Sam's brain. She discussed the scans with the radiologist.

"Do you think that's just swelling?" Wehby asked.

He studied the scans. He didn't want to commit himself, but he thought it looked like there was a significant tumor in the posterior fossa.

Reading a scan is as much an art as a science. Now, having slept all of twenty minutes during the last twenty-four hours, Wehby tried to understand what was happening in the boy's brain. He'd come out of the shunt surgery just fine. The scan showed that the shunt was in place and the ventricles were being drained of spinal fluid. Did he have smoldering edema, swelling? Or was he suffering a stroke, not getting blood to portions of his brain?

Normal intracranial pressure is 5 to 15 millimeters of mercury, and Sam's reading was more than 40. There was so much swelling, so much blood, that it seemed impossible to tell what was tumor, what was blood, and what was just swelling. But Wehby knew that Sam's brain stem was being compromised.

She considered operating. In a normal case, she would remove the portion of the cerebellum that was infarcted, and that would relieve pressure by giving the brain room to expand. But the mass was wrapped around the back of Sam's head, and to reach his cerebellum, she'd have to cut through the mass. She would encounter tremendous bleeding. The boy would die long before she reached the cerebellum. She felt so damn helpless.

She showed the scans to her partner, who had joined her. "What do you think?" she asked.

He stepped back and shook his head. "Blood's everywhere. There are no good options."

"Could I operate?"

"No chance."

Wehby studied the scans once more.

"There has to be something."

"No."

"So what do I do?"

"You tell his parents he's going to die."

Doctors call it "hanging the black crepe"—their way of preparing parents for the funeral. A surgeon comes from a hospital room, leaving behind weeping parents, and tells his partners: "I hung so much black crepe in that room that you can't believe it."

Monica Wehby didn't mince words when she gave parents bad news. That was part of being a pediatric neurosurgeon. Kids die. When Wehby told parents what the future held, she sometimes thought of her cousin, a twenty-year-old murdered by two men he'd taken fishing. His killers beat him, tied him up, threw him in a lake, and made off with his pickup. She thought of his mother, the pain she must have felt knowing that her son had needed her but that she could not be there for him. She knew the pain she felt when one of her own children's feelings were hurt. She couldn't fathom the pain parents felt when their child died, when a future was measured in months, or in the case of Sam Lightner, hours.

More than anything else, Wehby wanted to be there for her patients—the children. She remembered one family so distraught that they couldn't stand being at the hospital during the last few hours of their son's life. Wehby was haunted by the thought of this child dying alone. And so she sat in Intensive Care with the child in her arms, stroking his face and softly talking to him for several hours, until he stopped breathing. She considered it an honor, if that was how fate would have it, to help a child make the transition from this life to the next.

She didn't know the Lightners. She hadn't built up a relationship with them that grew through extended office visits and nervous moments in the waiting room. But she knew they were parents, and she was bringing them the worst news of their lives. As she went to find them, she planned to do what she did with all families: be honest and prepare them for the worst, but never extinguish hope until she was sure the child was not going to make it.

She found the Lightners talking with Sam's pediatrician. Dr. Davis had come to the hospital to check on Sam before going to his office. Wehby led them all to a cramped room in the scanning office. She stood by the scanner console and pushed buttons so the images of Sam's brain would come up on the monitor. She wanted his parents to see what was going on in Sam's brain.

"Hydrocephalus isn't the issue anymore," she said, and explained that she was going to return with Sam to the operating room to replace the internal shunt with an external one and thus make sure the pressure on his brain was not from spinal fluid. With the new shunt she would be able to see the fluid run off, and thereby rule out any shunt malfunction.

"The problem is with his brain stem." Wehby pointed to the images on the monitor. "He has all this swelling in there. At this point, I can't tell if it's a tumor, if the tumor has invaded his brain, or if it's a stroke. All we can do now is ride it out. I have no idea what's causing all this bleeding."

She pushed a button and a new image appeared on the monitor. "There's bleeding in the cerebellum and pressure on the brain stem. He has a lot of pressure. I can't operate."

Wehby let her words sink in. Her gut feeling was that the rest of Sam's brain—the cortex, areas of higher function—was fine. The cortex housed the soul, so to speak, the elements that made up his personality. This wasn't a case in which a kid suffered a severe head injury, as in a car wreck, and his entire brain was damaged. Sam's cerebellum could take a hit and compensate. The key was pressure on the brain stem.

"My goal is to take care of the rest of the brain and see if the stem can tolerate this pressure," she said. "He's not great. He's very sick. He's in critical condition."

This mother of four gathered herself. "I have to tell you," she said, "there's a good chance he could die."

The words hung in the air, and the Lightners started crying.


Wehby finished putting in the second shunt just before seven-thirty. She was aware that news of Sam Lightner's collapse would be in the paper, and she could just imagine how readers would see the story: "This kid goes through a dramatic surgery in Boston and then comes home, only to be killed by a local pediatric neurosurgeon. If he'd been in Boston, he'd have survived, but this stupid Portland doctor didn't know what she was doing."

But she couldn't dwell on this now. It was time for the next surgery. She glanced at the white board near the charge nurse's desk to see what operating room she was assigned to, then went to find the parents in the preop holding room, parents who knew nothing about Sam Lightner, who had no idea of what their child's doctor had gone through during the last twenty-four hours. They were there because they expected her to work miracles on their child. She took that child in her arms and disappeared into the operating room. And again Dr. Wehby got to work.

The turn of events had left the Lightners reeling. There were practical matters to deal with: Debbie and David both called their bosses to say they wouldn't be at work. And they had to break the awful news to those closest to them. Debbie called her mother. And then her neighbor Laurie, who had volunteered to let Emily and Nathan stay again overnight.

"No, Laurie," she said, "the kids need to be with us."

Emily came to the phone.

"Emily, don't go to school," her mother told her. "Someone will come and get you. We need you to come to the hospital."

She hung up and called Nathan's school. She spoke to someone in the office and explained that Nathan had to leave school. She was patched through to his classroom.

"Nathan," she said, "Laurie is going to come get you. We need to see you and Emily."

In time, Emily and Nathan arrived at the hospital. Their parents met them near the ICU, where family and friends had started to gather. The Lightners walked into an unoccupied room with sliding glass doors. They closed the doors and pulled the curtains for some privacy.

"Guys," Debbie said. "We need to be here."

She and David were crying.

"Sam is really sick," she said. "He might die."

"We have to be prepared that Sam's not going to make it," David said. "He isn't going to make it."

The four Lightners were all crying, all hugging one another. And then they slid the doors open and walked to the room where fourteen-year-old Sam Lightner, the boy behind the mask, lay dying.

**20** Monica Wehby compared surgery to an opera: some parts were slow and routine, others full of high drama. The first incisions would be the easy part of today's case, which was expected to last at least five hours. Even on minimal sleep, Wehby didn't feel tired. The lights were bright in the operating room, and the outside world and its mundane troubles disappeared; it was like being on the floor of a casino. The nurses, surgeons, and anesthesiologist were a team facing an unspoken truth, and again the casino analogy applied: They were gambling with the patient's life. Even in the simple cases, things could go bad. That truth always hung over the operating room.

Once they reached the center of today's surgery, Wehby would be unable—and unwise—to focus on anything but the patient. Her partner would count on her judgment and advice, as well as her unsurpassed skill with the surgical tools. Before then, though, Wehby had to know how the Lightner boy was doing. She asked the circulating room nurse to call the ICU for a condition update. The news remained bad: Critical.

Wehby knew that the boy was in good hands. But she was a realist. In the hospital, and soon within the greater medical community, Sam Lightner was her patient.

In the operating room, the opera was about to begin. The atmosphere changed. People didn't talk. The only sound came from the heart monitor, emitting its steady beep. Wehby made herself forget about Sam temporarily—and it was, curiously, easy. Years of training, of being under intense pressure, had taught her how to focus on what really mattered at any one moment. She turned her full attention on the child in front of her, knowing, as always, that in the waiting room down the hall anxious parents were counting on her to do her best for their child.

She leaned over the operating table and offered words of support to her surgical partner as he carefully cut into the back of the child's neck with a scalpel.


David and Debbie Lightner walked from the hospital room into the area where Emily and Nathan sat with friends who had come to support the Lightners. The updates from the ICU had been gut-wrenching: Sam wasn't expected to survive. Earlier in the morning, his parents and siblings had stood by his bed and held his hand, kissed him, and said good-bye.

Debbie flopped down in a chair. She hadn't slept all night, and was dazed. Her friends asked her if she needed anything. She shook her head and stared at the doors leading to the ICU.

David stood against a wall nearby. In one sense, he wasn't surprised to be at the ICU on a morning when he should have been at work. If Sam had been a normal boy, this would have been a shock. But for all these years David and his wife had known that some medical problem might strike down their oldest son.

David believed in God. He didn't believe God had caused this to happen, but he was convinced it was part of some larger plan. His family was in a crucible that would test their resolve and faith. More than anything, they had to believe in the courage and strength of the frail boy in that room, the kid who'd gone through so much during his life, the kid whose life now hung in the balance.

Tim Campbell made his way through Pediatric Intensive Care, checking his patients. As he approached the nurses' station, he noticed the Lightners outside one of the rooms. He asked a nurse what was going on, and learned what had happened during the night. The rumor was that the vascular malformation on Sam's face had roared to life and burrowed into his brain—practically a death sentence. If that was so, Dr. Campbell knew, the boy wouldn't live through the day.

Campbell approached the Lightners and followed them into Sam's room. At the foot of the bed he halted. The boy looked terrible, far worse than he had the year before. What he saw now shocked Campbell. He'd seen Sam weeks earlier and been impressed with the work of the Boston surgeons. Campbell offered his sympathy to Sam's parents and left the room. He returned to his office and phoned Dr. Jennifer Marler in Boston.

Marler, who was at home, was surprised to hear her pager. Her fellowship with the Vascular Anomalies Team had just ended, and although she continued to work in the lab, now that she no longer operated, she wasn't paged much. She was trying to determine the next step in her career, and was looking for a hospital where she could be both surgeon and researcher. There were no immediate openings at Boston Children's, and she knew she might have to move out of the area to find it. She looked at the number on the pager, baffled by the area code and number she didn't recognize. She called the number and remembered Tim Campbell's voice.

"Sam's in trouble," he told her.

"What?"

"He's in trouble," Campbell repeated. "I want you to know about it. Here's a number you can call."

Marler immediately phoned the ICU at Emanuel. A nurse filled her in, then went to find Debbie Lightner. Debbie came to the phone and told Marler that a Dr. Monica Wehby was in charge of the case.

Marler wrote Wehby's name down. She offered Debbie her prayers, and told her she'd let Dr. Mulliken know about the turn of events. She'd try to keep in touch throughout the day. After the call Marler sat in her living room in shock. Patients died or had complications after surgery, that wasn't unusual. What bothered Marler was the fear that she was responsible for what was happening to Sam. Was his Boston surgery somehow related? She was the one who'd pushed so hard to bring him to Boston Children's. She'd lobbied Mulliken to operate. Her fingerprints were all over this case. She couldn't stand the thought that her aggressiveness might cost a child his life.

Later, Marler contacted Wehby. She told her that she would bring Sam's case up that night at the weekly Vascular Anomalies meeting. She hoped the team could think of a way to help Sam.

Wehby—under pressure with a patient not expected to survive the next twenty-four hours—said fine. But privately she held out no expectations. She knew of Mulliken. His studies and cases were featured in some of the medical books on her office shelf. Yet brilliant as he was, Mulliken was a plastic surgeon. Sam's problem was in the brain, which was not an area of Mulliken's expertise. Wehby told Marler that any advice would be good, and welcome, but more than anything she needed the scans that had been done when Sam was in Boston.

The word at Emanuel during the past week was that surgeon after surgeon in Portland had always said an operation was too risky. Doctors and nurses agreed that the Portland surgeons had been right, but the all-knowing attitude at Harvard and its pediatric teaching hospital, Boston Children's, had led doctors there to take unacceptable risks.

Wehby didn't know what to believe. She hadn't gone back to read the newspaper stories on Sam. She didn't plan to search for them. Dealing with critically ill patients was hard enough without knowing about their hopes and dreams.

That evening, on her way to Boston Children's, Marler tried to remember the preop scans that had been ordered when Sam had come to Boston in April to be evaluated by Mulliken. He had been scanned again in July, just before the operation. The team hadn't seen any malformation invading the skull base. But that didn't mean anything. Malformations were a mystery, and they often expanded into new areas after surgery. Marler remembered removing a malformation from a boy's chest in the first of two planned operations. A year later, when it came time to work on the other side of his chest, an MRI scan showed a new mass that hadn't been present earlier.

As she left the parking lot for the hospital, Marler began crying. She didn't want to cry in front of her male colleagues, to be seen as weak. In the elevator, she wiped her eyes and composed herself; she had to look—and be—professional. She walked into the library, the same room where she had argued so hard to bring Sam to Boston. She hoped she'd done right. She walked to the front of the table.

"Before you start," she said, "I want to give everyone an update on Sam Lightner."

Some of the people in the room had no idea who she was talking about. So many kids passed through the hospital that their names were forgotten, or they became virtually anonymous. Marler had a photograph of Sam to show them.

"As you may remember," she said, "he's this young man from Portland, Oregon, who was operated on here in July. He's had a neurological event of some kind."

What advice, Marler asked, could the team provide to the pediatric neurosurgeon? She was passionate about her own silver bullet: anti-angiogenesis drugs, those that in studies on mice had stifled the growth of blood vessels that supplied cancerous tumors, and had thereby controlled the tumors. If the mass was in fact growing into Sam's brain, Marler maintained, it would be new growth, which could respond to the experimental drugs. She advocated using three such drugs on Sam.

The team didn't buy her argument, and some members were worried about using experimental drugs on a boy in critical condition. What if the drugs themselves killed the boy? And it concerned them that Marler wanted to use three separate drugs at the same time. Standard procedure was to use one, measure its effectiveness and side effects, and then try another. But the boy was dying, Marler said. She appealed silently to Judah Folkman: The boy was hovering near death, the drugs could give him a chance. That logic swayed the team, and Marler said she'd pass the advice on to the doctors in Portland.

On its front page the next morning, *The Oregonian* reported that Sam Lightner was in a coma. The terrible news stunned readers not only in Portland, but also across the United States. The story noted, incorrectly, that Dr. Tim Campbell had surgically inserted a shunt to drain fluid from Sam's brain. Campbell, of course, had had nothing to do with the shunt, and her fellow surgeons teased Wehby, asking her when Campbell had become a neurosurgeon. She laughed along with them, thankful that it was Campbell who was in the spotlight.

In the pediatric ICU that morning, Debbie Lightner told Wehby, "This isn't right. You should be getting the credit."

"No," Wehby replied. "It's okay."

Wehby called Boston Children's, looking for Marler, seeking answers on exactly what *had* transpired in Boston. She was connected to Marler in her lab. Once the pleasantries were out of the way, Wehby got to the point.

"Did you see anything in the pre-surgery scan?"

"No," Marler said. She explained how Sam had come to Boston after she'd been so moved by his picture in the file Dr. Campbell had sent. From the passion in her voice, Wehby could tell that Marler felt Sam was a special patient. Clearly she cared for him. But that really didn't matter. Wehby had to make sure he didn't die.

Had the team done any blood vessel studies to see if there was blood flow from the brain to the mass of tissue? she asked Marler. No.

Had the team done an angiogram, a test in which dye is injected into an artery so that an X-ray image reveals the condition of the artery, and then, as the blood drains, the condition of the veins?

Marler responded that the team hadn't thought it necessary, that the doctors knew the nature of the malformation and its location in relation to other structures.

Wehby thought that the brain *had* to be involved with this malformation. Blood flowed in veins through the brain and to the tumor. The venous drainage system in the brain would be affected by surgery that altered the blood flow in the malformation. When the plumbing in Sam's head changed, the blood found a new route. As Wehby figured it, this was a problem not with a tumor, but with the veins.

If it was a tumor, Sam was dead. If it was the veins, Wehby believed, this boy had a fighting chance.

**21** The first letters arrived at the hospital on October 6, the day Sam turned fifteen. Hospital officials forwarded them to the pediatric ICU, where Debbie and David Lightner were sleeping, waiting for news of their son. When they awoke, they began looking at the many messages from people they didn't know.

In one of the letters, the writer admitted weeping when he read about Sam's life and his quest to be normal. Sam, the writer said, was an example of "courage and determination," and was far from normal, in the best sense: he was "extraordinary . . . a shining star in an otherwise grey and dismal world."

The Lightners passed the letters to each other. They were touched by the words of a seventy-three-year-old man who wrote that Sam had reminded him what he never should have forgotten: to "look and really see the person you are looking at."

Sam's parents were surprised that anyone would bother to write their son. They were moved to read that people noted in Sam "a strength that most of us would never be able to find within ourselves." Sam was encouraged by one well-wisher to "let that inner strength and beauty get you through this."

Debbie Lightner set the letters aside. She thought about all the birthdays she had planned for Sam. All the cakes and candles, all the presents over the years. Her firstborn had turned fifteen. Would this be his last birthday?

Nurses continually monitored Sam's vital signs. A ventilator breathed life into him. On this most special of days, Debbie decided her son needed a gift. She brought him a stuffed animal—something he would have been embarrassed to be seen with had he been at home. She pried open Sam's seemingly lifeless hand and wrapped his fingers around the animal. She slipped the toy into bed with him, next to his body.

Throughout the day, more letters were brought to the ICU.

"I have had a difficult time concentrating on my work this week, as I have followed your story and thought deeply about all it represents. Thank you for the gift you have given us all by making yourselves vulnerable to cameras and reporters so that we might benefit from your courage and honesty. I am so sorry for all the pain you have had to endure—both physical and emotional—but grateful for the wisdom, patience and growth it has produced in you. You have so much to teach us."

Balloons were delivered to the ICU. Cards. And more letters.

"You have enriched our lives with your story. Not only, ironically, because of your bravery in dealing with your birth defect, but because you have helped us understand our own 'normal' son and daughter, who share your simple and basic wish for acceptance and understanding. Thank you for that."

That evening, two of Debbie's closest friends came to see her. David had gone home to check on Emily and Nathan, who were staying with neighbors. It was late, eleven p.m., and the three women sat in Sam's room. Debbie shared some of the letters with her friends.

"To the strong little man who has touched my life. Prayers and thoughts are with you and your family."

One friend had smuggled in a bottle of wine. She uncorked it and poured three glasses. They raised a toast to Sam.

When her friends left, Debbie stood by her son's bed. He should be studying for his learner's permit. He should be at school. He should be complaining about homework. He should be hanging out with friends.

The next day and after, Debbie and David sorted through more letters. They learned that in addition the hospital switchboard had received hundreds of calls. *The Oregonian* reported that it had received more than five thousand e-mails and telephone calls in only a few days.

There had been moments when the indignities of Sam's life especially saddened his parents. They watched him move through the world—dealing with people's stares and comments—and wondered where he got such strength. They wondered whether they could be as strong as he appeared to be. They wished that he could understand how he had touched so many lives. His goal in opening up his life to the newspaper had been to show that he was just a normal kid who wanted to be accepted for who he was. He wanted everyone to see the boy behind the mask. And now his parents knew he'd done just that.

After spending entire days and nights at the hospital, David changed his schedule, now going home to take care of Emily and Nathan at night. He would return in the morning and take Debbie home so she could shower. Then they would both go back to the hospital and sit beside Sam. When Emily one day asked her mother when she was coming home, Debbie was reminded that her other children needed her too.

At home, the Lightners realized that Sam's drama was being played out publicly. Neighbors who had never spoken of Sam asked how he was doing. Everywhere the family went in Portland, people recognized them as Sam's parents. At the grocery store, cashiers would see Debbie's name on a check and ask if she was Sam Lightner's mother. People in line would hear the name. And soon everyone would be asking about Sam, passing on best wishes. The attention was too intense for Debbie. She started refusing to go to the grocery store. She didn't know what to say to people. Sam was sick, desperately sick, and when the telephone rang she feared it was someone at the hospital telling her that he was gone.

When they arrived at the hospital each day, Debbie and David brought more letters, those they had received at home. They talked to Sam, trying to get him to respond, to emerge from the coma. They held his hands and stroked his hair. And when they ran out of things to say, they would pull up a chair and read from the letters, letters with similar themes; letters stating simple lessons that the writers believed should be followed always: acceptance, tolerance, openness, and tenderness; letters thanking Sam for giving "a better perspective on life and how it should be lived."

The nurses would check on Sam periodically and then leave the room, giving the family as much privacy as possible.

One night, when she had finished reading to her son, it occurred to Debbie Lightner that she didn't know how to plan a funeral.

**22** Dr. Wehby pulled big sheets of what looked like negatives out of an envelope. Each was about the size of the front page of a newspaper. She clipped them to the view box on her wall and switched on the light. She leaned forward, her face inches from the film. She was looking at images of the most mysterious organ in the human body—the brain. Sam Lightner's brain.

In medical school, budding neurosurgeons learn that the brain is the first distinct and identifiable feature in the embryo. After the union between sperm and egg, cells form a ball that eventually will become a human. During gestation, the ball develops a cleft that resembles the edge of a lima bean. That cleft eventually deepens, and one end will be the brain, the other the spinal cord. The brain hides its secrets. In a sense, it's like a circuit board in a computer, running on electricity and carrying messages and impulses through pathways. But unlike a circuit board, where it's easy for an engineer to see the individual components—the resistors and conductors—the brain has no spaces. It's as if thousands of circuit boards had been fused together.

Wehby was trying to determine why Sam was in critical shape, near death. Reading a scan involved sensitivity as much as science. There were scans that told stories of hope and relief. She'd read them and walk with a light step into the examination room. Others contained horrific news. In those cases, she'd deliver the verdict with compassion and honesty, as she herself would want if she were the one waiting to learn her child's fate.

The clues Wehby sought were hidden in the shadows of Sam's brain, tucked away in the gray areas on the scans. Some problems were obvious: Blood showed up as white. A white ball meant a hemorrhage. But in many instances, the scan was comparable to a piece of artwork. The interpretation was open for debate.

Wehby saw that the shunt she had inserted to drain the buildup of spinal fluid was working. Tests revealed that Sam's brain was still under severe pressure, however. The malformation might be the culprit, as it worked its way into Sam's brain, but Wehby didn't believe the problem was a tumor. Sam's mother had told her that he had been feeling sick for about a month. He had first had headaches, which grew progressively worse. Then nausea and vomiting. Finally, he couldn't walk without assistance.

Wehby believed Sam had been experiencing edema, or swelling, in the brain. That had progressed, probably in the last twenty-four hours or so, to an infarct, or a stroke. In order to survive, the brain needs blood—it's the conduit for oxygen and nutrients to the cells. Blood leaves the heart through arteries and is filtered to capillaries, where the oxygen is released. Blood and waste products drain into veins that flow back to the heart, and the cycle repeats. Wehby theorized that the problem in Sam's brain could be traced to the veins. She suspected that he had had a venous infarct. If an artery is clogged, blood can't get to the brain and the result is a stroke; part of the brain dies. If a vein is clogged, capillaries, which need nutrients from the blood to stay alive, weaken and die. If Sam's brother punched him in the arm, the punch would damage capillaries. Blood would ooze into surrounding tissue, later revealing itself as a bruise, and the arm would swell slightly. When blood leaks into the brain, the brain swells and causes pressure because the skull prevents the brain from expanding. That pressure, in turn, kills healthy regions in the brain, and the result is more bleeding. This cascading effect can be fatal. If there's too much pressure, the heart can't push hard enough to send blood to the brain. Coma, and death, result.

A venous infarct is hard to see on a CAT scan. Veins don't show up because their density is no different from that of the brain. Wehby had to study the scan carefully, looking for little specks of white, indicating blood, that would show she was on the right track.

The white specks would tell her Sam's problem was in the cerebellum, the area of the brain controlling his fine motor skills, his balance and coordination. A problem there would explain his difficulty standing. It would explain his headaches and confusion. But even if she determined this, the mass made it impossible for Wehby to operate and relieve the pressure.

Sam faced two dangers: His brain stem could be stroking— bleeding. On the scan, stroke and swelling looked the same, and it was impossible to know exactly what was happening. If the stem was bleeding profusely, Sam would die. Minor bleeding would cause cell death and limit recovery. Or, if the stem remained intact, the cerebellum could be squeezing against it. The swelling could not have occurred in a worse spot. The stem was Sam's hard drive—it ran his body. Pressure could choke the stem in the same way two hands around the boy's neck could squeeze the life out of him.

This case could go one of three ways, none of them good. Sam could die. He could remain in a coma. Or he could recover just enough to be locked in, his good upper brain trapped. He'd feel every human emotion, but be unable to move anything but his eyes.

Would it be more humane to prepare his parents, tell them that they might have to consider taking him off the ventilator and letting him go?

Or should Wehby fight at all costs to keep him alive? If she did, Sam might be in a coma for the rest of his life, shipped off to a nursing home. Wehby had seen cases of babies like that. They'd been abused, their brains destroyed by severe shaking. And God forbid, what if Sam survived, but remained locked in? That, Wehby believed, would be a fate worse than death.

She switched off the view box and put Sam Lightner's scans back into the envelope. Other patients were waiting.

"It's not a tumor," Wehby told the Lightners when she found them later in the ICU. She explained her theory: The removal of large sections of the vascular anomaly was successful but may have altered the blood flow within Sam's brain. That caused the swelling, and eventually, a venous infarct.

Debbie didn't know what to believe. She'd been thrust deep into yet another medical mystery involving her son. It had taken her nearly fifteen years to understand vascular anomalies. And now she had to learn about the brain. She thought about the images she and David had seen the night Sam arrived at the hospital. They peered over Wehby's shoulder as the images appeared on the monitor, one after another, black-and-white pictures that made no sense. And all the new words: *internal occipital crest, infarct, foramen magnum.* Through everything, her boy was dying.

The Boston handiwork was being undone. Sam's face was swelling grotesquely. His tongue, pushed out of his open mouth, looked like a cow tongue at the butcher's.

"All we can do is ride out the swelling," Wehby said. She wrote orders for the ICU staff to put Sam on steroids—the "holy water" of neurosurgery, which help reduce pressure. Dr. Marler had suggested anti-angiogenesis drugs, to cut off the blood supply to a new tumor. Wehby had the ICU use them, but after she concluded that they were not helping, they were discontinued.

"My plan is to take care of the rest of Sam's brain and see if his stem can survive the trauma," she told the Lightners. "You get most of your swelling in the brain three to five days after the injury. I'm going to try to get him through those days. I want to get him out past the stroke."

**23** Wehby played with a cotton ball, pulling it apart until a small tail hung from one end. She leaned over Sam's bed and held open his right eyelid with two fingers. She lowered the tail into the corner of the eye and dragged it across the white toward the pupil. If Sam blinked, it meant his cranial nerve was intact. There was no response. That's how Sam had been for days. The last report indicated that the boy rested quietly with his eyes partly open. There was an occasional blink, an occasional downward movement.

But Wehby had seen him respond to pain stimuli that she applied to his fingers, chest, and toes. And she believed he had once blinked when she asked him to do so. Even though no one else saw the responses, or could duplicate them when they examined Sam, Wehby thought the boy would survive.

She wanted to keep him in a finely tuned state of dehydration. His output of fluid, from his urine and the spinal fluid still being drained, would be measured. Only a minimum amount of fluid, obviously an amount necessary to keep him alive, would be replaced. The danger was that his body could take that as a signal to shut down. Wehby had to monitor lab reports and vital signs constantly, altering the drugs given to Sam and their dosages. At the end of four days, nothing had changed. Sam remained in a coma.

The Lightners asked that someone explain to them the interior of their son's head. They still couldn't visualize the brain. Photographs in a book were flat and confusing. The jargon tossed back and forth by the doctors and nurses was incomprehensible. Someone tracked down an anatomical model and gave the couple a basic lesson in brain anatomy.

Wehby still had no answers. Sam's heart rate, controlled by the brain stem, was fine. But he couldn't breathe on his own. That meant the stem was still under pressure. His temperature shot up to 105 degrees, then fell back to normal. Wehby detected more swelling in his brain.

All anyone wanted to know from her was whether Sam was going to live.

And all she could say was, "I don't know."

As she had told the Lightners, the most dangerous time in this new plan was the first three to five days. They were past that now, and nothing had changed. People in the hospital could count. Some had come to see Sam as a living corpse, being kept alive by a machine.

Not Wehby. For her, there was something there. And since she was in charge of his brain, the boy had a chance.

---

On a morning she had yet another seven-thirty surgery, Wehby hurried into the pediatric ICU. Shift change was from seven until eight, and the nurses cleared relatives from the ward then. At this time, Wehby could examine Sam, then be on her way in minutes. If she ran into the Lightners, she'd stay for an hour, an hour she really couldn't spare. In the evening she made sure that Sam was the last patient she checked on; she'd remain at his bedside for an hour, usually missing dinner with her children.

The Lightners were her eyes in the unit. Each nurse had to care for a number of patients. Sam's parents did nothing but look at Sam. And they knew their son better than anyone in the hospital. They spent hours talking to him, reading to him, stroking his hands and face. Each night, Wehby asked them if they'd seen any movement, any response at all. They told Wehby that there were moments when it seemed as if Sam had moved. It was subtle: a slight movement of the shoulder, a twinge in an arm or a leg. They just *sensed* something, even in eyes that everyone else might think cold and lifeless.

In the hard world of medical science, there's often not much use for feeling and intuition. Doctors rely more on a test result that they can analyze, measure, or hold in their hands than on a feeling that stirs within their heart. Matters of the heart are not to be trusted; a heart, after all, is vulnerable and can be broken, and is often tucked away in an inaccessible secret garden.

No one truly understood Wehby. People saw her obvious skills in the operating room. They appreciated her logical mind, her determination, and her stamina, which allowed her to stand beside a patient for hours at a time. But thinking like scientists, focusing on the dry facts, they missed seeing what she guarded so closely. What made Wehby a great doctor, what separated Wehby from her peers, was not just her hands and medical know-how. It was her heart.

What she offered the Lightners was hope. A pat on the shoulder or a smile. Her attitude, her quiet confidence, led them to believe with her that the fight was far from over.

She had no proof. There was no scan she could read. Maybe it was the angels, the kids who had died during her career, and who now watched over her. In that heart of hers, she believed not just in the power of medicine, but also in the power of Sam Lightner.

Wehby faced a different kind of pressure from what she encountered in the operating room, where her decisions were seldom if ever questioned. Now everyone—doctors, nurses, attendants—had an opinion on what should be done for Sam Lightner.

The scuttlebutt at the hospital, as Wehby knew, was that she was leading the family on, giving them false hope. She should be honest, her critics muttered, with the Lightners. Their son had been in a coma for more than two weeks. He had major problems in the brain. He was not going to get any better.

In any illness involving a severe head injury, there is an opportunity for a doctor to allow a patient to die by withdrawing support. In this case, it would mean disconnecting the ventilator that kept Sam alive by breathing for him, withdrawing care and letting the infections that were always ready to pounce take over and ravage his body. That decision—one ultimately made by the family—is excruciating, but it may be the most humane a parent can make.

Parents were always guided by Wehby's advice. Doctors tell themselves that they are only presenting the facts, but Wehby knew that parents could be influenced by the way the facts were presented. If she told the Lightners that Sam had no chance—if she laid out the scans and the textbooks and the case histories—they would feel that the most compassionate choice they could make for their son would be to let him die.

If Wehby missed her opportunity with Sam, he might survive the swelling but move into a vegetative state, in which he could live for decades. He would be what doctors call a gome. And no doctor wants to create a gome. As damaging as it was to offer false hope, Wehby considered it worse to remove all hope prematurely. Unless she was one hundred percent positive that Sam would not survive, she could not advise the Lightners to let him go. Sam's brain was functioning. His stem was squashed, but the cortex was fine. The risk, though, was that in encouraging the Lightners to maintain the faith, Wehby could create a situation where Sam might have been better off if he had died.

As stressful as the operating room was, Wehby had a sense of certainty there. She could see a tumor. She could adjust a tethered spinal cord and give a child a new lease on life. At her disposal were myriad surgical tools, teams of nurses and assistants, and the best of modern technology. But with this case she may as well have been trying to hold smoke in her hands.

Instead of rushing out of the ICU, Wehby went to look for the Lightners.

No test results. No lab reports. Just hope.

"There's no harm in waiting," she told them. "Sam will let us know what he wants us to do."


The multidisciplinary progress records on Sam were grim: *"There is real uncertainty if this is a reversible process that needs time or a progressive terminal condition."*

Only his parents and Wehby thought otherwise. Members of the medical community understood how the Lightners couldn't give up. But to them, Wehby was another matter.

Her critics felt that she had refused to face medical facts, and had crossed the line separating faith from foolishness. Not only that—she was a woman. Dominating the surgical world were men who prided themselves on being dispassionate. Wehby, they would say, was the classic woman who became too emotionally linked to her patient to see the truth. A tenet taught in medical school and reinforced during residency was that doctors must keep an emotional distance from their patients.

Wehby was getting ready for her seven-thirty surgery when an anesthesiologist pulled her aside. He had been in the male surgeons' locker room and overheard some of them talking about Wehby. "We all know the kid is not doing well," one surgeon had said. "She hangs on to those things. That's just how she is. We know all about her."

And then an ICU nurse told her that people were saying that Wehby was giving the Lightners false hope.

That kind of talk made Wehby boil. "I'm seeing what I see," she told the nurse. "That's what I believe. People think I'm crazy, but I'm not. And I'm not going to say that because no one else sees it, then I must be wrong."

The consensus was that when Sam died, or was carted off to a nursing home for the rest of his life, Wehby would move on to the next case. When that day finally arrived, the emotional brunt would fall to the Lightners because of Wehby's recklessness. Within the hospital, there was a sense that two tragedies were unfolding. One in the pediatric ICU, and another whose story line was still being written.

*"The patient has had waxing and waning neurologic status. However, his best status reported during the week, yet seen personally by this examiner, was some movement to command of his toes and possibly*

*his right hand. Most of the time, however, he has what appears to be reflex movement of his feet, no movement of his upper extremities. He has pupils that are unequal, with the left being at 3 and the right being at 2, and both are not reactive."*

Sam's parents returned to work, and tried to lead a normal life. But everywhere were reminders of a crucial piece missing. Debbie walked upstairs, looked into Sam's empty room and wished she'd find his clothes tossed on the floor. David saw the motorcycle posters hanging on his son's wall and wondered whether he'd ever feel the boy's arms around his waist as he accelerated into a turn. Emily and Nathan missed even the bickering among siblings. Even Maggie the dog seemed lost, and wandered the house looking for Sam.

At the bank, Debbie was expected to be cheerful and greet a steady stream of customers, many of whom knew about her family's ordeal. All day long she heard, "Hi, how are you?" But no one really wanted to know, and the bank didn't want her to tell the truth. So instead of saying, "Fine," which would have been a lie, Debbie said "All right." The Lightners kept one foot in the medical world—maintaining vigils at the hospital—and one in a world that was familiar, but somehow no longer real or, at times, even important.

In the midst of this, the Lightners discovered love: love for one another, a recognition that in being weak together, they found a common strength to carry on, to push forward day after day, but also love from family, friends, and even strangers. People came over and did laundry and straightened up the living room and kitchen. A neighbor made sure that Nathan wore clean clothes and combed his hair for his school picture.

Letters and cards continued to arrive at their home. One correspondent, an inmate at a maximum-security prison, told them he and fellow inmates had read about Sam and discussed what Sam had taught them about life. Teachers used Sam's life in classes as a way to explore subjects of growing up and feeling accepted. The Lightners found it strange to have their son described in such heroic terms. Even more puzzling were letters from parents who referred to the Lightners as special. They considered themselves an ordinary family dealing with an extraordinary problem. And the love they felt for their son, Debbie and David thought, was no stronger than the love any parent would feel for a child.

Each afternoon, the Lightners drove to Emanuel with more letters for Sam.

"We're here, Sam," Debbie would whisper in her son's ear. "Take your time. We're waiting for you."

*"For most of the time, he lies quietly with no spontaneous movement."*

"You do whatever you need to do to get better," she would say. "No matter how long it takes."

*"The next problem, and ... his major real problem, has been ... neurological. The patient's family are extremely attentive and have been at his bedside, talking at length with medical staff all week, and they do fully understand their son's precarious position, but are maintaining optimism as staff have advised them to do, given that he may recover consciousness and return to a comfortable life at home."*

All his life, Sam had overcome obstacles. He was a fighter; he took on the world, forced his way into the middle of it, and never backed down. On the drive to and from the hospital, his parents reassured each other by saying that Sam was in yet another fight.

His brain remained swollen—long past the time when a venous infarct should have subsided.

*"Overall, Sam has not had a week where much change has been noted."*

He couldn't breathe on his own, but occasionally his body seemed to struggle to breathe, and that disrupted the ventilator's settings. Some ICU staff believed that this was a death rattle, that the medical technology was only prolonging the inevitable.

His parents disagreed. After all, Wehby had noticed responses. The Lightners were convinced that Sam heard them and was fighting for his life. They told him they loved him. They never used the words "coma" or "death" in his presence. That would signal doubt, which could lead to defeat. They filled him in on what was happening at home and farther beyond the hospital walls.

David regarded his son with the same care he applied when making intricate pieces of jewelry. He said he saw things: a movement, a grimace.

"I know he's in there," he told the nurses.

Official progress reports told a different story: *"He does not open eyes to voice or noxious stimuli and does not follow commands to move arms or leg. No positives."*

Dr. Wehby wasn't making things any easier with her claims of seeing responses. She continued to spend time in his room at the end of each day, watching his body, monitoring his vital signs and reviewing lab reports, familiarizing herself with the boy's mysterious rhythms. He seemed to sleep during the day and have a slightly higher response rate at night, often as late as nine. Other doctors, however, asked Sam to move his toes, waited, and left the room; on his chart they noted: *"No response."*

Some nights Wehby stood over the bed and yelled: "Sam, it's Dr. Wehby. Can you move your toe?"

She would wait patiently. Sometimes nothing happened. But

sometimes, perhaps a minute or two later, his toe moved. Was it spontaneous? Or had Sam responded?

To make him respond, there had to be a significant, even painful, stimulus. Wehby would lean over his bed and grind her knuckles into his chest. With all the tubes and lines running into his body, with all the drugs being given to stop pain, Sam was in effect under general anesthesia. She had to do something to his body that was extremely painful. She saw that he always responded to these stimuli.

Wehby believed in Sam also because it made medical sense. Scans showed there was nothing wrong with the upper part of his brain. He should be able to hear, to think. The problem lay in getting the message from that portion of his brain through the compromised stem and out through the nerves.

Friends told her that an increasing number of doctors and nurses grumbled about her stubbornness: "I can't believe we are putting up with this," they would say. "She needs to let him go, and let the family get on with their lives."

As the days passed, the critics grew more vocal. Wehby's partners who covered for her on the weekends, checking on her patients, would see Sam's name on her list and ask how he was doing. "He's starting to follow some commands," Wehby would tell them. Later she would read the notes they had written while they were covering for her: *Exam unchanged, not following commands. Continue present care.*

Her critics wanted Wehby to have a frank talk with the Lightners and persuade them to consent to withdraw care. Yet Wehby wasn't on some absurd crusade. She was Sam's medical advocate, trying to do the best thing for him. That was an easy mask to wear in the hospital. She was Dr. Monica Wehby, acclaimed surgeon with a professional reputation others had to respect.

On the drive home each night, she faced her toughest critic, however—herself. Was she truly helping Sam? Or was she helping to create a totally devastated child? She'd watched families deal with the death of a child and move on. That was almost impossible if the child lingered in a nursing home, a living shell, a constant reminder of what should have been. Maybe she *was* prolonging the boy's misery. Did she want a good outcome so badly that she was imagining things?

Her answer had to come from within. And it was filtered through a soul that blended science and faith. Some parts of her life she held in her hand. Others were unseen, nothing more than a force that entered her and moved her heart. And in the medical world, logic and rational thinking always carried more weight than did passion and emotion.

Wehby was a Catholic, and her faith—while tested during the years she'd been a pediatric neurosurgeon—remained strong. That a human grew out of a couple of cells inside another human was a stunning accomplishment. The body was a complex machine. Things went wrong. In Wehby's view, there was no all-powerful God micromanaging life and deciding who got a tumor and who didn't.

Some surgeons were brilliant in the operating room, but incapable of relating to a person who wasn't anesthetized. Getting to Wehby's heart wasn't easy. There were numerous doors and locks. Her job didn't allow her to wear her heart on her sleeve. But clearly, she hadn't sold out that part of herself just to be excellent with a scalpel.

On that drive home each night, she was allowed to feel a part of herself that couldn't be nurtured in a hospital. She thought about Sam Lightner with her head *and* her heart. Her head studied the scans, and she believed in the power of technology. Her heart felt something when she watched this boy. And she believed in that too.

Dr. Monica Wehby's strongest conviction was in the overriding goodness of the human spirit. She believed in miracles. And as a girl she had learned that a miracle was nothing but the right thing happening at the right time.

**24** During the last week of October, Wehby took a vacation. Other doctors might have flown to Hawaii or Sun Valley to escape the pressure of their work; Wehby instead stayed home, for her children were her first priority. She was a patient mother, and easily left the operating room behind. She got up with her youngest when he woke in the middle of the night, slept just a few hours, and made sure she could drive her two oldest sons to school in the morning. Later in the day she watched the boys shoot baskets in front of the house, and made elaborate plans to decorate the house for Halloween. Because she was so good with her hands, she was able to create intricate spider webs out of spun cotton.

But Sam Lightner was never far from her mind. Each day she called her office for any news on him. Her assistant seemed evasive during one such call, and told Wehby not to worry. Wehby hung up, called the ICU, and asked to speak to a nurse. She learned there was a move under way, now that Wehby was at home, to persuade the Lightners to approve withdrawing support. A doctor who was convinced that Wehby was wrong had asked that an older respected neurologist be brought in for a detailed brain study that could be given to the family.

Wehby returned to work and headed off to a full day in the operating room. Between cases, doctors and nurses casually asked her about Sam. Wehby felt they were doubting her judgment. And then, finally, came the question: "Monica, do you *really* think he's going to make it?" She would nod, refrain from long explanations, and get back to work.

Late in the day, Wehby pulled Sam's chart and looked at the notes she'd made not even a week earlier: *"Occasionally following commands. Pupils are reacting. Positive. Gag."* She read the notes others had made while she was on vacation: *"No corneals. No gag. No cough. No response to pain."*

The latter observations made Sam Lightner sound damn near dead. There was a note from a neurologist who had been contacted by the ICU: *"Because of the variation in clinical observations we need some hard numbers that we can follow, hard objective data."* Wehby learned that the neurologist had examined Sam on a "fact-finding" mission. He had not discussed his findings with the family. He suggested a group exam so that a number of doctors could discuss their findings.

The Lightners mentioned to Wehby that a neurologist had tested Sam, but they hadn't heard about any results. Further, they said that Sam had responded to them while she was on vacation. The professionals be damned, Wehby thought. She believed the parents. And she believed in herself.

Wehby had kept Sam Lightner alive. The doctor and the boy

were linked. Whatever happened from now on would be traced back to her.

On November 10, 2000, the pediatric ICU filed its last report: *"Over the last month he has had a variable neurologic exam and at times was following simple commands such as moving his toes . . . but he has never been alert or fully responsive. . . . [He] is stable enough for transfer to the pediatric ward. His ultimate neurologic outcome is not certain, but a recent MRI showing suspicion of infarction of the brain stem area gives him a poor chance of good recovery, and his neurological exam may not improve at all from its present state."*

# the boy

## I'm the One Who

BY NATHAN LIGHTNER

*I'm the one who sees Sam laying in the sand filled hospital bed.*
*The one who sees the dimly lighted room of the ICU.*
*The one who sees the doctor telling mom & dad what's wrong.*

*I'm the one who hears the "beep" of the heart monitor.*
*The one who hears the nurses talking about their patients.*
*The one who hears the visitors talking quietly amongst*
*themselves in the waiting room.*

*I'm the one who believes Sam will survive.*
*The one who believes I will be away from hospitals for the*
*   rest  of my life.*
*I'm the one who wants my brother to be away from this place.*
*The one who wants Sam out of his wheelchair.*
*And most of all I'm the one who wants Sam to never be*
*   stared at again.*

**25** David and Debbie Lightner backed out of the room to let six nurses crowd around their son's bed. The nurses would be moving him twenty yards, from the ICU to the pediatric school-age ward in another wing. Although he remained in a coma, his vital signs were stable, and he no longer needed the round-the-clock care he'd received since he slipped into a coma. A neurologist had suggested a series of tests: auditory brain stem evoked response, somatosensory evoked potential, and visual evoked potential. But there was too much electrical interference from the machines in Sam's room to conduct the tests. If necessary, they would try in the pediatric ward.

Debbie watched as a nurse pulled from a wall socket the electrical cord that ran from the ventilator that kept Sam alive. Her eyes met the nurse's. "Don't worry," the nurse said. "This runs on a battery. Sam will be just fine."

Other nurses disconnected the suction tubing, and the monitor that kept track of Sam's heart and respiratory rates and blood pressure. The lines were reconnected to a portable monitor perched at the foot of the bed. Even for this short trip, nurses needed to know what was happening in Sam's body. A respiratory therapist waited in the hallway. He would walk beside the bed and constantly monitor vital signs. If Sam stopped breathing, the therapist was charged with keeping the boy alive.

A nurse lifted the ventilator—a gray box the size of a small computer printer—onto a metal cart. Debbie was once again amazed that such an unassuming device was her son's lifeline. During the commotion, she'd hoped that Sam would respond to the noise and activity. But he did not. During the last few weeks, there had been moments when Debbie wondered whether Sam would ever recover. Maybe she and her husband were fooling themselves. If she doubted, David was strong for both of them. "I'll tell you when it's time to worry," he would say. Then a few days later he would be the one needing reassurance and a calm hug from his wife. In the face of growing medical evidence, it was hard for either to believe that Sam would ever again look them in the eye, hold their hand, or laugh.

The only person who did not waver was Dr. Monica Wehby. She noted that it appeared Sam had tried to wink his right eye in response to a command from her. That would happen one day, but then for more than a week nothing would happen. In her reports Wehby described a waxing and waning in Sam, as if he were fighting to respond. Some professionals thought the eye movement, if it even was that, was random. It hadn't been consistent enough to be labeled a response.

At weekly care conferences held in the ICU, the Lightners listened to doctors and caregivers allude to the possibility of Sam's death. Out of respect for his parents, they would never come out and say it directly. No one used the word "death," but the Lightners, who had come to understand medical terminology and read between the lines, knew what was being implied.

Wehby's critics wanted someone to step forward and prepare the Lightners for something that seemed inevitable. Several times they were asked whether they wanted to continue to full code status on Sam. If his heart stopped, the staff inquired, did they want him revived? Debbie and David always said yes. But were they doing what their son would want?

Wehby had seen the eye movement. And so the Lightners clung to her words. If the ventilator was Sam's lifeline, then Wehby was the Lightners'.

The nurses, now on either side of Sam's bed, turned it and rolled it past parents so concerned about their own children that they didn't bother to glance up. Other nurses pushed the IV poles, and the cart holding the ventilator. They moved slowly, frequently checking the monitor to make sure that the trip wasn't putting stress on Sam's body. As the bed approached the doors leading out of the ICU, Debbie wanted to turn back. There was no denying it had been rough here—this is where Emily and Nathan had come to say goodbye to Sam when it seemed clear he would die—she was now afraid to leave. She knew all the nurses. She took comfort that the level of care given to Sam here was the best in the hospital. She didn't know what lay beyond those doors.

A nurse cleared a path through the hall. Visitors waiting to see patients in the ICU glanced down at the child in the bed and turned away in shock. Sam's head had swollen larger than at any time in his life. It nearly hid the pillow on which it rested. His eyes were open, but lifeless. His tongue—the size of a man's closed fist—extended a good six inches out of his mouth. His gums and parts of his tongue were black.

The nurses pushed Sam's bed down a ramp, stopping every few feet for the therapist to check the monitor. They headed for room 3509, the room closest to the pediatric nurses' station. Because he needed acute care, the supervisor had assigned Sam to this room; the location would allow the nurses to check on him.

A nurse wrote down the time of arrival on Sam's chart. Someone could walk from the ICU to his room in less than thirty seconds. Sam's trip had taken thirty minutes. His parents stood by as nurses hooked up the machines. One of them checked Sam's vital signs.

Once he was settled in and his parents had gone home, a nurse at the station flipped through Sam's medical charts and recorded his data. She then reached up to a white board and with a colored marker wrote the vital contact information: Primary doctor—Steve Davis. Consulting doctor—Monica Wehby.

A nurse who had been there the day Sam was born now came to hold his hand. "Sam, whatever you decide to do is okay with me," she said. "I'm here for you. I care for you. I want you to know that."


Stephanie Morris arrived for her morning shift, checked in at the nurses' station, and learned that she'd been assigned to Sam Lightner and one other patient. Although floor nurses usually cared for three patients each, those assigned to Sam had only one other patient under their charge, because he needed constant care.

Morris knew all about Sam—he had been on the ward for weeks—yet she still followed proper hospital procedure and called up his patient profile on the computer. He remained in a coma—a big concern to the rotating group of nurses assigned to care for him. They had taken to calling themselves Sam's posse. When replacing one another in shifts, they'd talk about this kid. Morris had told the others that caring for Sam had changed the way she felt about nursing. The others agreed. Most children spent just a couple of days on the ward before going home. Sam had been here long enough to become a part of their lives, even part of their family.

They were protective of the boy in room 3509. No one but a doctor could do anything to Sam without checking with them. And even then, the nurses stood by and kept watch on anyone who so much as touched Sam. His eyes, though open, were vacant and lifeless. Yet his nurses told one another that at fleeting moments it seemed he was aware of their presence. His one good eye didn't track them as they moved around the room, but he looked at them differently. At rare moments the eye appeared to glimmer. Most of the time, however, there was nothing; even so, the posse treated Sam as if he were conscious of all that was going on around him. They kept the television on. They spoke to him as they would to anyone.

Morris stopped in front of Sam's room and opened the pulldown box on the wall. She glanced at the flow sheet, the paper detailing Sam's vital signs and lab results. Everything looked good. The nurses had to watch for infections that might prove fatal if not caught quickly. The night-shift nurse briefed Morris on Sam's condition: Unchanged.

"Good morning, Sam," Morris said as she walked into Sam's room. The scar around his neck was oozing, and she changed the dressing. She wiped down his tongue and swabbed it with an ointment to help it heal. She stood by the side of his bed and made her first neuroassessment of the day.

"Sam, blink."

Nothing.

"Sam, squeeze my hand."

Nothing.

"Oh Sam, do something."

Morris combed the boy's hair and washed his face. She wanted him to look good for his parents. She believed in preserving his dignity. As she moved about the room and adjusted tubes and wires, she explained what she was doing, so as not to startle him. If he was at all aware of what was happening, he might be scared.

"So how did you sleep?" she asked. "Me, I slept crummy. I need more coffee."

She looked out the window. "It's a nice day, Sam."

Before she went to the next room to check on another patient, she took Sam's hand in hers. It felt lifeless.

"Sam, if you're going to be like this for the rest of your life, what do you want?"

She stroked his hair.

"Sam, you're a big boy. Do you want lifesaving measures?"

The hand never moved.


In early December, Monica Wehby stared at the stack of reports covering her desk. She took a handful of Christmas chocolates from on open bag for a boost of energy, and picked up the first report. She punched a number on the phone and began reading as fast as she could. When she examined patients, Wehby wrote notes, but she dictated reports for others to transcribe. As usual, she was behind in her paperwork. She could handle nine straight hours in the operating room. But paperwork instantly made her tired. She'd find excuses to put it off, until she'd have to come in on the weekend and do nothing but paperwork.

After completing two reports, Wehby closed up her office and went to check on Sam Lightner. The other reports could wait. It was always more rewarding to deal with patients. She'd finished her rounds, but wanted to see Sam before going home, for a change at a reasonable hour.

"Sam," she yelled. "Can you blink?"

Nothing.

She picked up his right hand.

"Sam," she called loudly. "Sam."

She leaned closer to his face.

"Sam, I want you to squeeze my hand. Squeeze it, Sam."

She waited.

Nothing.

And then . . .

A slight, an ever-so-slight squeeze.

"Sam," she repeated, "squeeze my hand."

*"He did it!"*

Nurses ran into room 3509.

"He did it!" Wehby yelled again. "Sam squeezed my hand."

She called Debbie, who was at home alone, doing laundry. Debbie rushed to the hospital and took her son's hand.

"Sam, squeeze my hand," she told him.

Nothing. She desperately wanted to say she felt something. But she had to be honest. "He didn't do anything."

Debbie leaned over Sam's bed. "It's okay that you couldn't squeeze. I know you're trying."

Now Wehby took Sam's hand. "Sam," she said, "squeeze my hand."

Nothing. Maybe it had taken all of Sam's energy to make that one feeble squeeze. But she was convinced of what she had felt. This was not about her, or her critics. It was about Sam. He was winning.

"I'm not giving up hope," she said. "This is a big victory. If you can get any movement, even a weak movement, in the arm or leg, it means the wiring from the brain to the body is still there."

But Wehby's report, which soon circulated through the ward, troubled Dr. Davis.

He went to see the boy.

"Sam, if you know I'm here, blink."

Nothing.

"Sam, squeeze my hand."

Again, nothing.

As the family pediatrician, Davis felt responsible not only for Sam, but for Emily and Nathan as well. He felt responsible for the entire Lightner family. The year was drawing to a close, and he found himself grappling with profound questions for which he had no answers. And they certainly wouldn't be found in a textbook.

What if Sam remained like this, blinking from time to time, but essentially trapped in his body?

Would he want to live like that? Davis remembered the kid who came to his office, the little wiseacre who liked to joke and talk about sports.

Is this what Sam would want? The question haunted Davis. *What would Sam want?*

When Davis encountered a neurologist in the hospital hall one day, he asked if he could spare a moment. Until two months before, Davis had known no more than the average pediatrician on matters of the brain. Now he was familiar with brain stems and nerve pathways. The simplest explanation for Sam's condition seemed to be that damage to Sam's brain stem had compromised his brain's ability to send commands to his body. It was like pinching a garden hose: the water wouldn't get through. Even though the nature of care was beyond Davis's expertise, he sat in on every care conference. He had nothing to add. But he listened, fascinated. He was hearing arguments from specialists who were increasingly pessimistic. Only Wehby, he noticed, wanted to stay the course. If Davis could have voted, he wouldn't have cast his lot with her. If he was going to be Sam's advocate, he needed advice. Good, solid, unbiased advice. He hoped the neurologist would give him some.

"This boy's been able to blink," Davis told the man, after outlining Sam's medical history. "That's it. What should we do for him?"

"He'll end up being locked in," the neurologist said. "He won't be able to swallow, or even move his mouth."

He paused and looked at Davis. "You want me to be blunt?"

Davis nodded.

"The best thing you can do for this boy is to do nothing. Let him go. Do the right thing. Let him go."

Later, in his office, Davis went to his computer, found a search engine, and typed in the words "locked-in syndrome." There were numerous hits. Davis began reading. His heart grew heavy.

*A person may retain consciousness and intelligent thought but become entirely paralyzed except for eye movements.*

*The disorder leaves the patient a complete mute.*

*The prognosis for those with locked-in syndrome is poor. The majority of patients do not regain function.*

*Like a mind in a jar.*

*Communicate by blinking Morse code.*

*Urine and bowel must be drained, victim must be turned and rotated frequently or ulcers will develop to destroy bone and muscle.*

*Cannot communicate needs or wants or discomfort. The victim's needs include companionship and the variety of daily experiences that any person would crave.*

Is this what Sam would want?

Davis called the Lightners at home. He spoke to Debbie, and asked if she and David could meet him in his office that afternoon. He had to talk with them privately, away from the hospital.

Davis thought about his relationship with the family. He'd grown close to David, who, he'd learned, didn't trust hospitals or doctors. In trying to find common ground during the time they spent together in the ICU, the two men found it easiest to talk about Sam. Davis learned more about the boy during those weeks than in all the years he had cared for him. He'd learned about his character, his fierce pride to fight his way into the world, and his contentment with the surgery to alter his face.

Once the Lightners arrived, Davis shut the door to his office and searched for the right words. The silence was awkward. It was so much easier to talk about ear infections or chicken pox. Yet they all knew why they were there, and Davis had initiated the meeting.

"As you both know, there's nothing more that can be done medically for Sam," he said gently. "He's stable. He's not getting worse, but he's not getting better and—"

"But he could," David interrupted.

"Yes," Davis acknowledged. "He could. That's true. Sam could get better, and that's what we hope and pray for. But in two months nothing has really changed. We have to face that fact. Nothing has changed with Sam."

He paused.

"Here's something you have to consider: If something catastrophic should happen to Sam, should we resuscitate him?" Davis continued. "When we've talked about it at the care conferences you've always been clear that you do not want to change the order to DNR."

Do not resuscitate. In the care conferences, death had been expressed in such clean, unemotional language.

"Is that the best thing for Sam?" Davis asked. "Is that the best thing for your family?"

He saw the shock in David's eyes.

"Everyone is doing what they think best for Sam," Davis said. "But we have to confront this."

"Yes," Sam's father said. "It is the best thing."

"I'm not sure," Davis replied. "The majority medical opinion is that Sam is not going to get any better. Let's say he improves just a little. He could be locked in, paralyzed."

He handed the Lightners some literature on the syndrome. "Is this how Sam would want to live?"

The Lightners glanced at the material.

"No motor skills, no nothing, and with the chance he would die soon anyway," Davis said. "He would have the ability to think and reason, but not to move or communicate at any level. Is that how Sam should live?"

David Lightner shook his head. "If he was in a vegetative state with no brain activity, I could see that. That's a different deal. But Sam has been blinking. I've seen it myself. He's going to get better."

Davis didn't know how to respond.

"Look," David said, "even if he ends up in this locked-in state, there are a lot of things he can enjoy. People, music, reading . . . He could be productive. Look at that Stephen Hawking."

Davis put his hands out and touched both the Lightners. He wanted to persuade them to take no extraordinary measures. If Sam's heart stopped, not to have it restarted. If an infection started to ravage his body, to let nature take its course, and not fight back with antibiotics.

"I think it is time," he said quietly. "I think it is time that we let Sam die."

David shook his head again. Now he was adamant. Damn the medical reports and the experts. David Lightner knew his boy. And his boy was a fighter.

"After all he's been through, I want to give him a little more time," David said. "Just a little more time."

**26** In late December, once it was clear he could breathe on his own, doctors began weaning Sam from the ventilator. His parents saw him try to move his eyes when they entered the room.

"Sam, can you see the TV from where you are?" his mother asked. His eyes moved up to the screen and then back to her.

A week later he moved a finger on his left hand, very slightly. His parents held his hand, asked him to squeeze, and felt a slight pulse. The squeeze was so weak that some nurses and doctors said they didn't feel anything. Wehby felt the movement.

"He's there," she told the Lightners. "He's telling us to just wait."

There were days when he would only blink, and days when he would squeeze on command. The changes in him were as subtle as the fading of the day. There was no magical moment, no dramatic turning point. He emerged as mysteriously as he had vanished.

His parents, overwhelmed with joy, yet still apprehensive, began contemplating a new way of life.

Wehby was emotionally and physically drained. Surgically, the case had been routine. But managing the aftermath had been like nothing in her career. Even in the most intense case, a child dropped in and out of her life, usually within a matter of days. Other children could be considered sprints. Sam Lightner was a marathon, testing her faith when those around her did not believe. This boy had reminded her of her best quality: her heart. She should never doubt her instincts.

Those in the hospital who had doubted her during the dark days faded into the woodwork. The doctors who had commented about false hopes simply shut up, saying nothing when they passed her in the hall. Wehby herself didn't talk about the case. She wasn't looking for a pat on the back. This wasn't about her vindication. As she saw it, she hadn't done a thing. If there was a hero, it was Sam Lightner.

Sam didn't know what to think. He remembered nothing of the coma. He wasn't scared, because there wasn't anything to be scared of. He knew he was in a hospital. His last clear memory was of being at the Imaging Center office with his mother, who was filling out paperwork. Since then there had been a thick fog, no sensations or memories. The first thing he remembered after that was the sound of Christmas music—a nurse had played a tape in his room. But he couldn't hear it clearly. One nurse told Sam he'd been in the hospital for three months. That seemed unreal. He felt as if he'd taken a long nap.

The hospital's speech and occupational therapists rigged up a pressure-sensitive device connected to a machine with programmed responses. Sam's father had them program a request similar to the one before: *I want a woman.* The first time Sam called it up, Dr. Davis saw the corners of the boy's mouth tremble. "Sam," he asked, "are you trying to smile?" Sam squeezed his hand.

He was happy to be alive. He appreciated little things: television news, rain beating against the window, and the sound of people laughing and talking in the hall outside his door. His family secretly brought Maggie the dog, and she curled up next to him. His parents lifted his hand and set it on the dog so he could pet her.

Friends came to see him, to tell him how things were going at school. Sam knew he wouldn't be going back. He was going to miss his freshman year.

Each day, his mind seemed clearer. He liked teasing with the nurses. He would try to laugh when they said he had a crush on Britney Spears, that he thought she was a "hottie." The nurses were right!

One afternoon, Dr. Davis came by with a woman Sam didn't recognize. Davis introduced his daughter. She wanted to be a teacher, and he had told her she had to meet an amazing child. Sam blinked a hello.

"Sam, I want you to tell me the story of when you were on the motorcycle with your dad," Davis said. "Squeeze my hand when I say how fast you were going."

Sam loved telling this story. No one believed him. But it was true. Davis started at forty-five miles per hour and kept increasing it. Fifty? Sixty-five? Eighty?

Sam suspected that Davis's daughter wasn't sure that he was even aware she was in the room. But he was quite aware.

"How about a hundred ten?" Davis asked.

Sam squeezed.

Trapped though he was in this bed, Sam felt he was once again becoming a part of the world. Members of Grant High's football team left a game ball for him at the nurses' station. Other students— none of whom he'd met—sent cards, which were hung on the wall.

He learned that the school paper had featured a story about him, and that teachers had talked to their classes about his struggles.

He watched television, and was able to control the set with a contraption the occupational therapists had set up, a small pressure plate that required only the slightest of touches to work, it could also summon nurses when he needed them. Sam liked the ability to change channels so easily when there were commercials. He followed sports closely. When a nurse asked about a particular football player, whether he'd done well on a particular team, Sam squeezed her hand yes in response.

Visitors who didn't know Sam invariably did one of three things: talked loudly, as if he couldn't hear them; avoided looking him in the eye; or spoke slowly as if he were stupid.

But he was there. He heard it all. He understood it all. By squeezing Davis's hand he let the pediatrician know that he was aware that, after all that confusion, George W. Bush was going to be the next president of the United States. The first time he broke out in a real laugh was when Nurse Morris mentioned that her cat had farted in her face.

In mid-January, Sam had been a patient for more than three months, longer than any other young person in the hospital. His extended prognosis was unclear. Rehabilitation therapists needed to help him regain some strength before he could be released. Davis suggested the family think of moving him to a nursing home while he recovered. The Lightners were firm on this: The only place Sam was going was home. They would arrange for home nursing care so they could go to work. Debbie and David would give Sam their bedroom on the first floor and take Sam's room upstairs. They had a ramp built so a wheelchair could be pushed in the front door. They repainted his new room, and he picked out the color, blinking his eye, squeezing their hands at the shade of blue he wanted.

But for now Sam was still in the hospital. Because he had been lying on his back for so long, Sam's body had not been obtaining oxygen where it was needed. He had no strength or endurance. The therapist's goal was to strengthen him enough to sit in a wheelchair.

"Do you want to get up and going?" the therapist asked him during one session.

Sam squeezed her finger. Four nurses gathered around his bed. He felt hands lifting him. He was lightheaded, dizzy. Three of the nurses held his body, the fourth held either side of his head. He felt her hands let go, and his head flopped to the side and down to his chest. Now he felt hands gently lift his head and hold it so he stared straight in front. After not even twenty seconds, he was exhausted. The nurses sensed he'd had enough for the day. They lowered him to the bed.

"It's a start," the therapist said.

The therapist and nurses measured his improvement in seconds. Sam graduated after sitting on the edge of the bed for a full ten minutes while someone steadied his body with two hands around his torso. Then it was time for the wheelchair. The nurses wheeled into his room a Stryker chair, a special platform wheelchair that they could slide him into directly from the bed. Once his body and head were secure, they could tilt part of the chair's platform into a seat back. Sam heard the explanation. He looked at Nurse Morris, hoping she would understand that he was scared.

"Are you excited?" she asked.

No response.

"Are you a little nervous?"

Sam squeezed her hand.

"Will you trust me?"

He blinked.

One day, while Morris was wheeling Sam through the ward, he

spotted Dr. Wehby. Her back was to him, and she seemed to be writing. He had heard about her from his parents, and had come to expect her evening visits in his room. Morris pushed Sam's chair to the station and stopped just behind Wehby.

She turned.

The doctor who had had faith when others seemed to have had none locked eyes with the boy who had desperately needed someone to believe.

He didn't know what to do.

And so he did the most natural thing in the world. He barely lifted his arm, and waved.


Sam was watching the news on television one day, when something caught his eye at the door. Nurse Morris stepped into his room. He saw that she was not in her uniform.

"I'm not scheduled to work today, but I had to come in." She took Sam's hand in hers.

"You're going home."

He blinked and squeezed her hand. Other members of Sam's posse joined her. They lifted Sam out of bed and onto the "boat"— a plastic device that allowed him to lie down while they bathed him. They dressed him, combed his hair.

"Sam," Morris said, "you're glowing."

She pushed him in his wheelchair to a room at the end of the hall. Sam looked up and on the wall saw a poster signed by his team of nurses:

"Sam, we already miss you."

"Thank you for all the laughter and smiles."

"Sam, you're the best. Just knowing you'll be thriving at home is wonderful."

"Enjoy. You've earned it."

His parents were there to present the nurses with a framed portrait of their family, signed "To the angels at Emanuel."

Sam didn't know who started crying first. But the nurses were. And so was his mother. A call came into the nurses' station. The ambulance that would take Sam Lightner home after 133 days in the hospital was ready in front of the hospital. His parents pushed him out of the unit. Nurses waved at him. Sam lifted his wrist to wave back. Nurse Morris walked with the family and helped the attendants get Sam situated in the ambulance.

She leaned toward him. "You're going to make it." She wiped tears from her eyes, turned and gave Debbie a hug.

"Thank you for letting us take care of your son."

27  The physical therapist had Sam squeeze her hand as a way of testing his strength. She took some notes. She was direct, and told Sam that if a boy his age lay in bed for two weeks because of an injury, it would take six weeks to regain his strength. And Sam had been bedridden for nearly six months.

"We're going to rebuild your body one step at a time," she said. "Are you ready to try?"

He squeezed her hand.

His balance was gone. He needed to learn how to control his head and his torso. And he had no strength. The therapist watched him struggle, reading his facial cues: a grimace, sweat on his forehead, and sometimes just a resigned sigh, telling her that he could not try one more exercise.

The strange thing was, his mind was all there. He'd get on the computer and e-mail his friends or use the instant-message function to carry on a conversation. He was witty, and wanted to know what was going on in school. But when his friends dropped by the house, there was nothing he could do.

Debbie would help him into his wheelchair and push him to the dining room table. His arm would rest on a table attached to the chair. His head would flop to one side. His tongue remained swollen and drool ran down his cheek.

A friend would look through a motorcycle magazine. "Hey, Sam you like this one?"

He'd put the magazine on the wheelchair table. Sam wouldn't move his head. His eye would flicker toward the page. Slowly he would raise his hand.

And then his friend would go home and Sam would be alone. It seemed as if he had lost a year of his life. His friends were making new friends. They were learning how to drive and going to dances and finding their way in high school. At night, with the television off and the house dark and quiet, Sam hated what he had become. No one could understand how awful it was to lie in bed awake and unable to move. There were moments when he felt angry. There were moments when he cried. At times he felt like quitting, unsure whether he had it in him to fight one more fight. All his life he had fought. And Sam Lightner was tired of fighting.

Then morning would come and he'd hear the physical therapist arrive. He had a choice. Stay in bed for the rest of his life. Or find a way to get out of this bed and this house.

"Ready, Sam?" the therapist would ask.

He'd start again.

At first all he could do was practice holding his head in one position. Or try to keep his stomach tight so his body wouldn't flop over when he sat on the edge of his bed. Eventually he was able to raise his arm over his head, and bring his knees to his chest and hold them for a few seconds.

One day his parents lifted him from his bed into his wheelchair. They strapped the seat belt around his waist and pushed him out the front door, down the ramp, and onto the sidewalk. At the end of the block, they turned. A few blocks farther on, Sam saw a crowd in a parking lot. People were waving at him and yelling his name. There was his posse! And there was Dr. Davis!

In the middle of the crowd were a bunch of motorcycles. Davis, knowing Sam's love of motorcycles, and wanting to pay tribute to the women who had cared for the boy, had contacted a local Harley-Davidson dealer. He told the manager what he wanted. The Rose City Hogs, a motorcycle club, agreed to bring their bikes to the parking lot. The Harley dealer let the nurses pick through his racks of biker apparel. Sam's posse was all decked out in leather. Sam thought they looked good. So too did a group of men watching from nearby.

"Sam," Dr. Davis said, "These are your angels. We're calling them Sam's Angels."

One of the Rose City Hogs got his camera ready. He was going to take a picture of the event, Davis said, and make it into a poster for Sam. Another biker spoke to Sam with particular interest. "I fell out of a hot-air balloon and the doctors told me I would never walk again," he recounted. "They were wrong. You're going to make it."

He helped Sam onto his motorcycle—a three-wheeler—and placed him in the middle of all the nurses. Nurse Morris moved in close. In her hand she held something few people might recognize. But she knew that when Sam eventually saw the poster he would get her little joke. She had sneaked the object from the hospital especially for this. Just before the photographer snapped the camera, she lifted an enema bag.

Throughout the summer, Sam worked at rebuilding himself. His goal was to return to Grant High School in September and regain the life he had sought. Doctors suggested he go to Emanuel for an intense five-week session to rehabilitate himself. Although he couldn't stand the thought of the hospital, he realized he had no choice. This would be his boot camp. While his friends were swimming or playing basketball or just hanging out, he would be stuck back in the pediatric school-age ward.

He brought his new poster to the hospital and all the nurses signed it for him. People he didn't know sent cards to his room. One couple stopped by and left an inspirational message on the board in his room.

One day when he saw Nurse Morris coming down the hallway, he backed his wheelchair into a corner of his room.

"Sam," she called when she entered the room. "What are you up to?"

Wielding a grabber—a pinching device he could control with one hand—he caught Morris on the leg.

"Sam!" she exclaimed.

He laughed and began coughing. He wheeled himself to his suctioning apparatus and cleared the mucus from his breathing tube. While he was in the hospital, the nurses regularly monitored him, but Janice Cockrill, a pediatrician specializing in rehabilitation, had devised a plan to make Sam responsible for much of his own care.

His case had been the most unusual in Cockrill's ten years at the hospital. She had first met him after he had come out of his coma. At the time, he could only move one finger. When Sam looked at her then, he couldn't control his gaze. Cockrill thought his chances of making at best a slight recovery were slim. By the time Sam went home, she had been amazed.

Now, on his return to Emanuel, Cockrill had set simple goals: he needed to regain his strength, try standing, take a few steps, and be able to live independently. That meant he had to be able to dress his upper body, brush his teeth, and go to the bathroom on his own.

Sam had hated the first few days at the hospital. Everything he had to do reminded him of what he had lost. He missed being a teenager. He was spending all his time with nurses—as nice as they were—who were a lot older than he was.

One morning he wheeled himself out of his room and down the hall. A nurse stopped him.

"Sam," she said, "you have to wear the seat belt."

He shook his head and sped away. His breathing was labored as he rolled toward the elevators that would take him to the basement for therapy. A trickle of blood ran from his nose.

"Hi, Sam," a doctor called to him.

He nodded.

Two nurses in the hall waved to him. His arm was too tired to wave back. He stopped for a moment to rest. An aide came from behind and put his hands on the chair. He started to push. Sam shook his head.

"You don't want any help?" the aide asked.

Sam nodded.

"You sure?"

Sam wheeled away.

Sam parked his wheelchair in a room the therapists called the gym. A therapist helped him stand and led him to the parallel bars, then helped Sam stand between the bars.

"I want you to take one step forward," she said.

Sam concentrated, willing his right foot to move. Then the left. He was breathing heavily, and blood flowed from his nose. The therapist wiped it from his mouth.

"Want to quit?" she asked.

Sam shook his head. He took another step.

"What I want you to do now is let go and see if you can stand."

He stood still for thirty seconds, then began to sway.

"Excellent, Sam. Nice control today. Try the squats."

He bent down four inches. Held the position, but fell as he stood up. He grabbed the bars and tried again.

"Sam," the therapist said, "you did awesome."

As he left the gym, he moved to one side to let a girl in. She was sixteen, a little older than he, and whenever Sam felt sorry for himself, he thought of her. She had been in a car accident and needed a strap to keep her head in place when she was in a wheelchair. She couldn't talk, just a few low moans, but Sam liked her and waved to her whenever he saw her. One day when she had regained enough strength in her head to not need the strap, Sam wheeled over to her and gave her a thumbs-up. He found a piece of paper and wrote three words: *Way to go.* He handed it to the girl's mother.

Sam's speech therapist gave him a small computer with which he could type out answers to people's questions. But he found pencil and paper to be far easier. The therapist also gave him all kinds of goofy exercises—putting his tongue on the inside of his cheek, pushing and holding it there.

In the afternoon, he worked with an occupational therapist, who had him get on his knees and attempt to throw a beanbag into a little hoop three feet away. Getting in and out of the wheelchair was part of the therapy, and by the time Sam picked up the beanbag, his arm was so tired it shook. One day he missed the first basket, and fell to one side and lay on the floor.

"How are you going to get out of that?" the therapist asked.

Sam scooted to one side and grabbed a bench with one arm. He strained to pull himself to a kneeling position. His breathing was labored. Blood ran from his nose. He started to choke. The therapist moved to help, but Sam shook his head. He found a towel on the floor and wiped his face. He pulled himself to a kneeling position and tossed another beanbag at the basket.

"Sam, you did great! You want to rest?"

Sam shook his head again and reached for yet another beanbag. He made two shots with his right and then switched to his left. He made two more. His arms trembled and the therapist reached under his arms to help him into his chair. Sam shook his head. He sat on the floor for three minutes. And then he pulled himself up, and slowly sank into the seat. He motioned for a beanbag. He wanted to make a long shot. He aimed carefully and let it fly.

Swish.

"You always want to end with a success, don't you?" the therapist asked.

Sam smiled.

The physical therapy was easy compared with the schoolwork. He was ahead of his class when it came to math, but the hospital teacher wanted him to obtain freshman credit for English and history. The teacher made him read about Africa and then locate all the national capitals on a map. It was hard to read the tiny letters, but he completed his assignment. And then she hauled out the book he would come to dread.

She pulled a chair up next to his wheelchair and began reading aloud from *Romeo and Juliet*. Sam's mind wandered.

"Sam, are you paying attention?"

He shook his head.

"And why not?"

He made a writing motion. The teacher set the book aside and searched for pencil and paper. Sam wrote two words: *Too mushy*.

One day a therapist pushed Sam to the doorway of the rehab gym. The sixteen-year-old girl who had been in the car wreck was inside, lying on a table, crying as a therapist manipulated her legs.

Sam wheeled himself into the room and motioned to a staff member for a piece of paper. He wrote something and pushed himself over to the girl. He handed her mother the note. He motioned to his mouth, indicating that she should read it out loud to her daughter. The therapist helped the girl sit upright, and held her so she could maintain her balance. The girl smiled at Sam. Her mother unfolded the piece of paper. She started to read.

"'I did it. . . .'"

She put her hand on her chest and started to cry. She wiped the tears and tried again.

"'I did it. You can too.'"

He gave his friend his customary thumbs-up sign and wheeled himself out of the gym and to the elevator. He had to go back to his room and gather his things. It was time to go home.

His mother was supposed to come for him at about three-thirty, and until then there was nothing to do but bother the nurses. He chased them down the hall in his wheelchair.

"Come on, Sam," Nurse Morris told him at one point. "No wheelies in here. All I need is for you to fall over, and then I'll be in real trouble."

He wheeled himself behind the nurses' station and stared at the patient board on the wall. Less than a year before he had been wheeled into room 3509 and no one on the ward thought he would live. During this recent stay he had been assigned to room 3540. He stared at the board, thinking about where he had been.

And where he was going.

He turned his chair and pushed himself over to Nurse Morris, who was just finishing a report. He tapped her on the shoulder.

"What can I do for you, Sam?"

He pointed to the board and wheeled himself back in front of it. He waved to summon her over, and gestured for paper and pencil. He wrote something and handed it to her: *Help me stand.*

She lifted him from the wheelchair. He stood on his own. He reached up to the space for room 3540 and rubbed out his name. He tottered, and Morris extended her arms to steady him.

"You want to sit down?"

He shook his head.

He reached down to the counter and picked up a colored felt-tip marker. He lifted his hand and in the blank space wrote: *Going bye bye.*

Morris smiled. She dug into her pocket and handed Sam a going-away card. "I'll miss your great sense of humor," she said, and reached down to give him a hug. "You have a great life, Sam."

And then Debbie Lightner arrived.

She pushed Sam down the hall. Nathan waited at the elevator. "It's going to be like old times," he said.

They pushed Sam into the elevator. A nurse saw them and asked, "You done?"

"We're done," Debbie answered.

And then the doors closed.

**28** As his parents pushed him toward Grant High School, Sam Lightner fought back waves of disappointment. This wasn't how he had imagined himself returning to school. But at least he was back. Even though he had missed all but ten days of his freshman year, Sam was listed as a sophomore, on track to graduate with his friends in the class of 2004. What had kept him going during those months of rehabilitation had been the goal of walking into Grant under his own power, blending in with all the other students. But he still required the wheelchair.

Debbie and David brought him to school an hour early on this September day. The school would be empty of students, and being alone would give Sam a chance to settle in and meet his assistant, a woman provided by the school to help him get around the building.

His parents pushed him into an office where the woman waited, and then said good-bye.

Later, from beyond the closed door, Sam heard the sounds of people in the hall. He heard them greet one another and slam locker doors. He wondered whether anyone would remember him. A few friends had visited him at home, but Sam hadn't been a part of this world for so long. He was anxious to find out whether he still belonged.

He glanced at the watch on his thin wrist, waiting for the first bell of the day. The schoolwork didn't intimidate him. The social world was another matter. The wheelchair made him different. And then again, there was his face. It remained swollen, and his tongue was distended, so it was impossible for him to speak. In his backpack, on the wheelchair, was a handheld computer that allowed him to type messages for others to read. He looked at the door. He told himself to relax.

The bell rang.

Sam grasped both wheels and propelled himself across the room. The assistant opened the door. Through the crack, Sam spotted scores of kids, his schoolmates. He hesitated, then summoned his strength and pushed himself out of the office and into their midst.

He saw them turn away, avoid his eyes, and walk around his chair. He didn't remember Grant that well, and the crowd disoriented him. Was he supposed to go left or right? He turned to the right, and nearly ran into someone.

Up ahead, he saw someone he knew, a girl from his middle school. She was with some other girls, all of them laughing. There was no way he could catch up to her. And even if he did, would she want to be seen with him?

On his way to his first class, biology, he passed his old locker. Another reminder of how life had changed. He had liked hanging out there, even if it was only briefly, talking with his locker partner Brian and getting to know some of the guys. Now, because he was in a wheelchair, he didn't need a locker: it was easier for him to carry all his books in his backpack the whole day.

He wheeled himself into the biology classroom. Everyone else seemed to have a friend. Sam sat quietly. He stared straight ahead, and didn't even bother taking out his computer.

His third-period class was on the second floor, and the school didn't yet have a working elevator. Sam wheeled himself to the base of a set of stairs and pushed himself out of the chair. His legs trembled, and he struggled to keep his balance. While he grasped the rail with his right hand, his assistant put her hands under his left arm. Sam concentrated, willed his left leg to take a step. And then his right. He dared not look to his left, because he knew he would lose his balance. But he could feel students rushing by, taking the steps two at a time. Finally at the top of the steps, he waited while the assistant went back down for the wheelchair. The journey had taken ten minutes.

At lunchtime, Sam wheeled himself to the nurse's office and fed himself a nutritional supplement into the line that ran into his stomach. With his swollen tongue he could not eat normally. He wondered what was happening in the cafeteria.

When his mother picked him up at the end of the day, she asked him how school had gone.

*Fine,* Sam wrote on his computer.

After a month of relative isolation, Sam had had enough of feeling sorry for himself. If the other kids didn't approach him, it was up to him to approach them.

Now when he wheeled himself down the hall, he waved. At first nothing happened, but after a week, other kids were waving to him first.

In class, he would raise his hand when he knew the answer. He would type it on his computer, and someone sitting near him would read it. Most of the time he was right. And it turned out that the kids in his class thought the computer was fun, and they argued over who got to read his answers. When his hands tired of typing, other students volunteered to take notes for him.

He noticed a cute girl sitting next to him in his American history class. After thinking about it for a while, he decided to be bold. He typed out a message and handed her the computer.

*Do you get what we're doing in here?*

She typed out a reply.

*No.*

They talked every day before class, usually about homework. Then Sam began asking the girl, whose name was Emily, what she'd done over the weekend. And then she started motioning for the computer so she could ask him about his weekend. Sam found he liked learning about American history.

One day, as he made the effort to leave his wheelchair and climb the stairs to the second floor, a group of boys hung around watching. He didn't know any of them, and he ignored them as he started the climb. He stopped to catch his breath.

"Good job, Sam," he heard.

He turned and saw two of the boys carrying his wheelchair to the second floor. They waited for him at the top of the steps. From that day on, the same boys carried his wheelchair upstairs.

He was in the main hall one afternoon when a boy on the cheerleading team came up beside him. Sam saw that he had a megaphone. The boy stepped in front of the wheelchair and lifted the megaphone to his lips.

"Make way for Sam," he announced. "Make way for Sam."

Over the months, something had changed at Grant High.

Now when Sam moved through the halls, students slapped his hands. They called out to him. In classes, they picked him first when it came time to work on group projects. There was talk about taking Sam off campus for lunch when the weather improved.

A year had passed since Sam was last released from the hospital. He wheeled into his American history class and looked up to see Emily standing in front of his desk. She smiled at him, and reached into her pocket and pulled something out. She set it on his desk.

"It's for you, Sam."

It was a red and white card, with lace attached. In the middle was a heart. He turned it over.

"Happy Valentine's Day," Emily had written. "I hope everything goes your way."

He looked up. He felt the heat on his face. He knew he was blushing.

She was still smiling.

And he smiled too.

# acknowledgments

I was at my desk in the *Oregonian* newsroom one day in late 1999 when my telephone rang. A reader familiar with my work said that he knew a Portland family whose son was horribly disfigured. He wasn't sure exactly what was wrong. The family didn't hide the child, but they were private and had never talked publicly about him or the life he led. If the family ever decided to tell their story, the reader said, I should write about this boy. I asked him to talk to the family. A week later, Debbie Lightner called and invited me to her home.

I went to the Lightners', and Debbie and I talked. She asked if I wanted to meet her fourteen-year-old son, Sam. She called his name, and I heard footsteps tromping down the stairs. I'd been a journalist for almost twenty-five years, and covered crime for a decade. That background didn't prepare me for the face that appeared in the doorway.

I'd never seen anything quite like Sam Lightner. Something deep inside me—the part of all of us that, despite evolution, remains an animal—was unsettled and scared. He didn't say a word. He sat in a chair and listened to his mother and me talk. After several days, Debbie called and said that Sam wanted to tell his story.

His goal was simple. He hoped that if people read about him they'd learn to see beyond this face.

He wanted them to see the boy behind the mask.

This book would not be possible without the Lightners, and I am in debt to them. Sam and his parents allowed me into their lives, graciously accepting my constant presence and never-ending questions for more than three years.

Sam faces ongoing medical problems and expenses. Plans for a second round of surgery at Boston Children's Hospital have been put on hold while he rehabilitates. His goal is to walk again without assistance, and he plans on attending college.

David Lightner has decided to follow his dream of designing and selling his own line of jewelry. Debbie Lightner continues to work at the bank to obtain health insurance. The Lightners have been deeply touched by all the letters they have received. They welcome correspondence, and can be reached at Box 13369, Portland, Oregon, 97213-0369.

I also thank: My wife, Barbara, and daughters, Rachael and Hanna, who put up with my absences during this project. I could not have written this book without their support.

My mother, Beverly Butterworth, who saw a future for me beyond a mediocre high school grade-point average and then showed me the path. My father, Tom Hallman, Sr., who gave me his gift of story.

My editor at Putnam, Aimee Taub. The third time really was the charm. As I told her, I believe in fate. She has been a great guide for a writer who wasn't always sure where he was headed.

My copy editor, Anna Jardine—a genius with the pencil.

My agents, Irv Schwartz and Noah Lukeman; our great relationship began with a simple cup of coffee.

My attorney, Ben Kaminish, the tough guy who looks out for the babe in the woods.

This book grew out of a series of articles that appeared in *The Oregonian* in early October 2000. I thank publisher Fred Stickel, editor Sandy Rowe, and executive editor Peter Bhatia for their leadership and vision in creating an encouraging and nurturing environment in which to work, and for giving me a leave to write this book—and taking me back. My editor, Jack Hart, is the best narrative editor in American journalism.

The staff at Boston Children's Hospital gave me complete access. Drs. Jennifer Marler and John Mulliken patiently taught me about vascular anomalies and, even during their toughest operations, let me peer over their shoulders and ask inane questions.

Dr. Steve Davis, whom I met in 1999, proved that a good doctor cares not just for the patient, but for the entire family. Stephanie Morris speaks for the unsung heroes among us—nurses. Doctors, nurses, and researchers in Boston and Portland graciously took my phone calls, and allowed me to pester them in the operating room, the changing room, and hospital hallways as I worked on this project.

In Portland, Dr. Tim Campbell generously took under his wing a writer who barely passed his science classes. It was the two-tone shoes, right?

Dr. Monica Wehby gave me her most valuable asset—her time. She showed me where medicine and faith intersect, and clearly demonstrated that the great ones combine head and heart. She convinced me that there are forces in life that cannot be explained.

# about the author

Tom Hallman, Jr., won the 2001 Pulitzer Prize for feature writing for a series of articles about Sam Lightner that was published in the Portland *Oregonian*. Hallman, who had been a Pulitzer finalist twice before, has received every major national writing honor for journalism, including multiple American Society of Newspaper Editors awards, a Scripps Howard National Journalism Award, a National Headliner Award, and a Nixon National Writing Award. A reporter for more than twenty-five years, Hallman has been at *The Oregonian* since 1980, and is currently a senior reporter specializing in features and narratives.